For more than two decades, Barry Farber has been bringing successful sales strategies to companies like mine. They all rely on two important elements—simplicity and creativity and this book has both.

—Arthur Wagner, President and Co-Founder, Active International

Farber and Shook use real-life success stories to demonstrate the best techniques to cut the clutter and strategically engage decision makers in a meaningful way to capture business. Their examples are ones every sales professional can execute and clearly show how thinking out of the box and really taking the time to understand your client's needs can make a world of difference in growing your business.

—Bonnie Habyan, Executive Vice President of Marketing, Arbor Commercial Mortgage

Farber and Shook combine their real world sales experience and entertaining stories with the top sales experts so anyone in any profession can benefit. Fast read and practical tips you can use right away.

—Bill Carigan, Vice President of Strategic Markets, Cintas Corporation

Farber has produced another hard-hitting gem that anyone serious about selling must read. It is years of real-world sales experience captured in an entertaining and useable guide.

—Jim Coriddi, VP, Dealer Division, Ricoh U.S.

Success Secrets of Sales Superstars offers a great collection of stories that are both engaging and memorable. Regardless of your industry or level of sales experience, you will find inspiration in this book. As Barry and Robert note—everybody sells.

—Isadore Sharp, Founder and Chairman,

Four Seasons Hotels and Resorts

A picture paints a thousand words and a story paints the road map. Farber and Shook deliver a powerful message on how building relationships, adding value, listening and execution will change the way you sell and get results. Great read.

—Dimitrios Smyrnios, President, Nestlé Dreyer's Ice Cream Company

I've always believed that the best sales strategy is to build relationships first and then do business. Barry Farber's new book takes this concept to the next level with great stories from iconic business leaders that are insightful, often amusing and always relevant.

—Jim McCann, Founder and CEO, 1-800-FLOWERS.COM

and Celebrations.com

This book is a must have if you're in any type of sales. Barry has put together an incredible list of people whose philosophies are game-changing.

—Mitch Modell, CEO, Modell's Sporting Goods and

featured boss on CBS' *Undercover Boss*

SUCCESS SECRETS
OF
SALES
SUPERSTARS

BARRY FARBER AND ROBERT L. SHOOK

THE MOVES AND MAYHEM BEHIND
SELLING YOUR WAY TO THE TOP AS
TOLD BY 34 INDUSTRY LEADERS

EP
Entrepreneur.
Press

Entrepreneur Press, Publisher
Cover Design: Andrew Welyczko
Production and Composition: Eliot House Productions

This publication is designed to provide accurate and authoritative information
in regard to the subject matter covered. It is sold with the understanding that
the publisher is not engaged in rendering legal, accounting or other professional
services. If legal advice or other expert assistance is required, the services of a
competent professional person should be sought.

Library of Congress Cataloging-in-Publication Data
Farber, Barry J.
    Success secrets of sales superstars: the moves and mayhem behind selling
your way to the top as told by 34 industry leaders/by Barry Farber and Robert L.
Shook.
        p.   cm.
    ISBN-13: 978-1-59918-502-6
    ISBN-10: 1-59918-502-4 (alk. paper)
        1. Selling. 2. Sales management. 3. Sales personnel—Interviews. 4. Customer
relations. I. Shook, Robert L., 1938– II. Title.
    HF5438.25.F374 2013
    658.85—dc23   2012023125

Printed in the United States of America

17 16 15 14 13   10 9 8 7 6 5 4 3 2 1

⋆ Dedications ⋆

Barry Farber
To my son Sam, who has taught me about persistence, never giving up, and the power of having a sense of urgency. I love you, Dad.

Robert Shook
To Jacob, Sawyer, Will, Jeremy, and Oliver. In my book, you are the world's greatest grandsons. With love, Papa.

Contents

* * *

Acknowledgments

★ ★ ★

There are many people to thank for their help and support in the writing of this book. First and foremost, our immense appreciation goes to the storytellers for their insightful and interesting stories. Each of them put a lot of thought into choosing his or her story, and consequently, we were able to put together what may very well be the greatest collection of sales stories ever told. Without our storytellers, obviously this book could not have been written. We thank you all for your participation. In our book, you're the greatest!

All of the interviews were recorded, and thanks, Debbie Watts, for doing the transcriptions. Debbie is professional and reliable—a great combination. She is always a pleasure to work with.

Our gratitude goes to Jeff Herman, president of the Jeff Herman Literary Agency. We appreciate his insight and the fine job he did in selling our book to Entrepreneur Media. Thank you, Jeff, for telling us a story for our book—and a very good one, "Resourcefulness."

We made a lot of new friends and we reacquainted ourselves with many old friends who work with our storytellers. These people are: Marty Abrams, Joe Arterburn, Matt Baldwin, Bronwin Barilla, Marilyn Brady, Beverly Brown, Misty Candreva-Martin, Patti Carr, Brenda Cooper, Kim Chow, Debbie Gobel, Michael Goldman, Debby Hatkins, Shawn Kelly, Likisha Jackson, Paul Kidwell, Peter Kofitsas, Lou Koskovolis, Charlie Lanktree, George Liang, Ed Lubin, Kelly Martin, Cara McManns, Danna Michael, Carol Noyes, Laura Reid, Jackie Skorvanek, Ron Spath, Blaise Tracy, Amy Vrzal, Shaun White, Dan Weinberg, and Joyce Wieser.

We had the pleasure of being able to work with some terrific people at Entrepreneur Media, who are: Ron Young, who heads the company's legal department; Randy Gil, our copyeditor; Karen Billipp, our editor; Leanne Harvey, director of marketing; and Jillian McTigue, marketing manager. We enjoyed working with Ron, Randy, Karen, Leanne, and Jillian, and much of the success of the book will rest on their shoulders. We anticipate they will do great things to help make our book a bestseller.

Last but not least, we thank our wives, Allison Farber and Elinor Shook, for the supportive roles that they play in all of our endeavors. We both feel blessed to have such wonderful women as our partners.

Foreword

by Jack Canfield

Author of the *Chicken Soup for the Soul* Books

I love a good story, and the millions of readers who have read my *Chicken Soup for the Soul* books know this. In fact, I built my career around storytelling. Also as a motivational speaker, I tell lots of stories, and judging from my audiences' reactions, I believe most people appreciate a good story, too.

Among the very best storytellers I've met over the years are the top salespeople I know. So when Bob Shook asked if I would write a foreword for his latest book, I willingly read the manuscript. Upon completing it, I was happy to comply with Bob's request. Not only is *Success Secrets of Sales Superstars* filled with interesting field-tested stories about selling, but also each of these narratives provides valuable tips on how to improve one's selling skills. It doesn't matter if you're a novice, a seasoned professional, or a high-powered CEO, this book is filled with gems that will benefit all readers.

Bob and his co-author Barry Farber both have successful sales backgrounds, and they know their subject well. Their selection of salespeople runs the gamut. They put together a collection that has a cross-section of top business leaders and highly successful salespeople—from America's top real estate people to two of the nation's most outstanding financial planners. They've even included a dynamic yacht dealer (who was born blind) as well as a matchmaker whose fees are as high as $500,000 for providing introductions to their future loved ones for her clients. There are also CEOs from two pharmaceutical companies, a toy company, a mattress company, and many more fascinating storytellers. Each story provides valuable insights that can be useful, regardless of what you sell. And we all sell for a living, even those of us who aren't making actual sales calls on customers. To a large extent, just how well we sell plays an important role in our success.

Each story is told in first person by the storyteller—and all are well written. My advice is that after you read each story, take the time to analyze and digest what you learned from it and, most important, what you can personally take away from it. I'll tell you one thing—each story is so enjoyable that once you finish it, you will want to keep on reading. It's like eating a bag of potato chips—it's hard to eat just one and stop without eating more! That's exactly what I found myself doing. It's a formula we applied when we wrote our *Chicken Soup for the Soul* books, and I know it works, judging from readers' reaction. With this in mind, I congratulate Bob and Barry for writing a book that's hard to put down.

My advice is to try not to read this book in one sitting. To get the maximum benefit, read a chapter, take some time to reflect on what you have read, and ask yourself, "What in this story can I do that will work for me?"

This is a book that is worth reading again and again. And perhaps that's the test of a truly good story. We enjoy it the second time sometimes even more than the first time. I think you will find this to be the case when you read these stories.

Foreword by Jack Canfield

Introduction

by Robert L. Shook

★ ★ ★

Barry and I met about 20 years ago and had an instant rapport. We both were authors and had successful sales careers. That's an unusual combination because the writing and selling professions are diametrically opposed. A writer is most productive when he is in solitary confinement, facing a computer screen, whereas a salesman's most productive time is when he's facing a customer. A writer's work requires an introverted personality; the salesman's, an extroverted personality. You could say that people like Barry and me are anomalies.

To be sure, when we get together, Barry and I usually talk about selling more than we do about writing. We enjoy exchanging sales stories, and we like to play the one-upmanship game, each trying to top the other's sales tale.

When we were having dinner earlier this year, Barry commented, "I recently spoke at a sales conference, and later that night I was cornered in the hotel lobby by a group of salesmen. They wanted to ask me questions and discuss sales strategies, the topic of my speech.

What followed was a two-hour session in which everyone took turns swapping sales stories. One of them said, 'I loved your talk today, Barry, but do you know what?' Before I could answer he added, 'The stories that were exchanged here in the lobby were the icing on the cake.'

"Everyone agreed with him," Barry said.

"I see that, too, when I attend sales conferences," I answered. "Not only does everyone enjoy those informal sessions, they are an excellent source for ideas."

"Those spontaneous stories are the gems you rarely find in books," Barry concurred.

"That's because the vast majority of salespeople aren't writers," I said, "so their stories rarely get written."

You can see where this conversation was going. That night Barry and I agreed to collaborate on *Success Secrets of Sales Superstars*. "With our combined sales and writing experiences," Barry said, "plus our contacts across the country with top salespeople, CEOs, and entrepreneurs, we will get the best sales stories ever told."

We agreed to be selective. Our criteria were

1. the story must contain a good lesson that the reader could emulate in his or her line of work, and
2. the story must be interesting and entertaining.

"We don't want to write a book that reads like a textbook," I said, "because nobody will want to read it. Let's make sure our readers enjoy every story. This way our book will be read cover to cover."

We elected to include "authors' comments" on the lesson(s) gleaned from each story at the end of each one. "If we can hold our readers' interest and teach them how to be better salespeople," Barry said, "*Success Secrets* will be a must-read for salespeople in all fields. It will also appeal to people whose job descriptions don't include selling to external customers. These readers also need to hone their skills when they sell ideas to their bosses, co-workers, and subordinates." Barry paused momentarily and added, "The fact is, everyone sells."

We have assembled an eclectic group of interesting storytellers. In *Success Secrets,* you'll be privy to some wonderful stories told by such people as Martin Shafiroff, America's number-one financial advisor and a legend in the securities industry; Bob LaMonte, a super sports agent who specializes in representing NFL head coaches; and Joyce Rey, who sells lavish homes with $20 million-plus price tags in Beverly Hills and surrounding communities. We also have stories from Dave Liniger, the founder and CEO of RE/MAX, a firm that has sold more real estate annually for the past decade than any other company in the world; Thomas Millner, president and CEO of Cabela's Inc.; Alan Levy, CEO of Cinchcast Inc.; Gary Fazio, CEO of Simmons Bedding Company; and Kerwin Elmers, the founder of Custom Coach. Over the years Elmers has sold million-dollar custom coaches to celebrities such as John Madden, Clint Eastwood, Paul Newman, Muhammad Ali, the Saudi Arabian royal family, and the Emir of Kuwait.

David Steward, the founder and chairman of World Wide Technology, the largest African-American-owned company in the United States, had a delightful story about how he first got started in business. Kevin Kelly, the CEO of Heidrick & Struggles, the nation's leading executive search firm, which places more CEOs and top executives with Fortune 500 companies than any other, told us a wonderful story about a breakthrough sale he made in Japan. You will also meet Vince Morvillo, a past president of the Yacht Brokers Association of America and a highly successful yacht broker in the Galveston, Texas, area who has been blind since birth. Another fascinating storyteller is Mark Roesler, founder and CEO of CMG Worldwide, a firm that mainly represents dead celebrities (their estates, that is). His 300-plus past and current clients include Elvis Presley, James Dean, Marilyn Monroe, Babe Ruth, Mark Twain, Sophia Loren, and Hugh Hefner. We even recruited our literary agent, Jeff Herman, to tell his favorite sales story.

Adhering to the principle that everyone sells, some of our stories are about internal sales. These are sales made to senior management and associates vs. outside customers. One of these tales features Roger

Newton, who is hailed as the co-discoverer of Lipitor, the all-time bestselling prescription drug in the world. This incredible statin, which reduces LDL cholesterol, was nearly canned by management and would have been, if not for Newton's dramatic presentation at an internal review board, a committee consisting of 12 senior executives.

Another great story about an internal sale is told by Neil Friedman, president of Toys "R" Us. Friedman's story dates back to 1995, when he was president of Tyco Preschool, a division of Tyco Toys. In this story, Friedman tells about how he pitched an advertising campaign to a group of Tyco executives who were reluctant to approve a sufficient budget to launch a new toy, Tickle Me Elmo. Using persuasive salesmanship, Friedman made the sale, and Tickle Me Elmo went on to become one of the most successful toys ever sold. You will also be privy to several other stories that involve internal sales, each illustrating why everyone—even though his or her job description makes no mention of selling—needs to rely on sales skills to achieve maximum success.

We urge you to read every story—try not to pick and choose only those tales directly related to your field. We give this advice knowing that salespeople are prone to exchange ideas and swap sales stories mainly with others within their industry, and as a consequence, recycle the same worn techniques that are used by their competition. As you will discover, *Success Secrets* offers useful, field-tested ideas from outside your area that can be used to sell to *your* customers.

With this in mind, we encourage you to think outside the box— be willing to cross-pollinate your sales techniques with those from salespeople who sell products and services that differ from your own. Alter these ideas to fit your product and service, and come up with something fresh and different that will dazzle your customers. As Oliver Wendell Holmes, Jr. said, "Many ideas grow better when transplanted into another mind than in the one where they sprung up."

During our research we heard a lot of stories, and not all of them made the final cut. Some had a good lesson but weren't interesting; others were entertaining but lacked substance. By turning down some stories, *Success Secrets* evolved into a wonderful collection of valuable lessons we are confident will be enjoyed cover to cover.

I have a confession to make: Barry and I initially agreed that we would not include our own stories. But we gave into the temptation, and each of us wrote one of our favorites based on our sales experiences. We applied the same criteria to our stories as we did the other 32 and hope you will find them as informative and entertaining as the rest.

Turning Dreams into Realities

Martin D. Shafiroff

Financial Advisor

★ ★ ★

M artin D. Shafiroff is an investment representative and managing director of Barclays Wealth. Based at the company's New York City headquarters, he joined the company in September 2008, when it acquired Lehman Brothers Private Investment Management business in the Americas. Shafiroff has been in the securities industry since 1966 and has been recognized as the top-producing financial advisor in the United States for more than 30 consecutive years. He heads a team of 15 financial professionals who serve and advise corporations, institutions, pension funds, and individuals, generating billions of dollars of transactions every year.

★ ★ ★

A while back, one of my clients referred a billionaire to me, a man who owned a coal mining company in the Midwest. I called and introduced myself to him. I asked him about his investments, and he said, "Mr. Shafiroff, you are wasting my time and yours if you try to sell equities to me. I have absolutely no interest whatsoever. I have 22 guys who are experts on bonds, and I'm satisfied with them."

"I'm not going to do that," I replied. "I would rather just be friendly with you and occasionally call to say hello. I have no desire to work with you in bonds because, at best, I am only mediocre in bonds. If your sole interest is bonds, we may never do business."

"I appreciate your being upfront with me," he said.

My comment seemed to take him off the defensive, and he then felt comfortable telling me about his successful coal company, which was his pride and joy. We talked at some length about business in general. Then I said to him, "Sir, what has been one of your greatest dreams in business?"

"You know, Mr. Shafiroff, I've always dreamed of owning a life insurance company. That's what I call a great business."

"Who knows?" I said. "We may be able to do business after all. Let me go back to my firm and see if the opportunity exists for us to start a life insurance company. If I come up with something that looks interesting, I'll get back with you."

"Don't you forget," he reminded me, "I have no interest in equities. So don't come back to me with how I can buy stock in a life insurance company. But owning my own life insurance company, now that's a different story. Yes, that's intriguing. I'll look forward to hearing from you, Mr. Shafiroff."

I extensively researched the life insurance industry, focusing on learning how to start one from scratch. I did a thorough study and even called some successful people in the industry who had founded their own companies. I also talked to others who tried and didn't succeed. I learned a lot from both sources. Then I came across a life insurance company that rejected a friendly takeover bid and consequently had a significant drop in its stock price. The stock was selling at less than 50 percent of its book value, and at that discount to book, I thought it was a tremendous value.

I sent the man a letter, along with additional documentation that explained what we'd have to do to start a life insurance company from scratch. Using a figure of $20 million to illustrate my point, I told him how we could form a company with that amount, which would be our book value. Then we would have to set up sales offices, hire administrative people and agents, establish departments for processing applications, handle claims, and so on.

"We'll also want an A+ rating from A.M. Best," I said, "and by the time we're ready to open our doors, we will have put $40 to $50 million into it. This investment will get us into the game as a regional company that does business in perhaps as many as ten states. We'll also have to put a lot of money into advertising because nobody will know who we are."

I took him through all the steps, emphasizing that all of this would make us a regional participant, but we'd have to be patient until we built up additional capital and experience to be a national entity.

After mailing the package to him, I waited a few days to give him time to digest it. Then I called him. "Did you have some time to review the information I sent you?"

"Wow, it's quite an undertaking to start a new life insurance company," he said.

"It is, but I have another possibility that might interest you," I explained. "There is a company on the NYSE called The Life Insurance Company. It is selling at less than half its book value. If we buy it on the open market instead of putting up $20 million for book value, we can accumulate the same dollar amount for $10 million. We won't have to go through all the startup procedures, hoping to get an A+ rating from A.M. Best, because it already has the highest rating. We won't have to recruit a management team or develop a sales force either. And the company is licensed in all 50 states, so instead of trying to build a regional company in 10 states we'd start off as a national company. The company is about 100 years old and is already well known, which will make it easier than to have to tell prospects we've only been in business for a few months but want them to make a long-term commitment to us."

He asked why it was selling at 50 percent of its book value, and I explained that it had turned down the friendly takeover, causing the price of its stock to take a dive.

There was a pause in the conversation. I waited so he could digest what I told him. I then asked, "Why pay two to three times as much to create something when we can buy a public vehicle—one that we can sell at any time—and receive a substantial cash dividend while we're waiting for the results?"

Remember now, this was a man who was strongly opposed to owning equities. Suddenly he saw the big picture, which was the tremendous discount and real value of going right into a position with a public company vs. the tribulations of starting a privately held company. After I showed him that equities could provide exactly what he wanted to accomplish, he no longer viewed the transaction as playing in the market, and neither did I. We viewed it as a means of entry into an industry at a giant discount.

Immediately following that conversation, the client bought a sizable equity position in The Life Insurance Company. Over a period of time, he accumulated more and more holdings. This excellent investment turned out to be the beginning of a long friendship; over the years I found other discounted bargains in which he took large equity positions. A few years later, he told me that his equity portfolio was larger than his bond portfolio. In reference to the life insurance company, he said, "You know, Marty, even though it trades like a stock, I don't view this investment as stocks." He also said that today he looks at his equity positions as values because they are businesses that cannot be duplicated for twice the price.

⋆ Barry's and Bob's Comments ⋆

By understanding his prospect's goal—remember, the client wanted to own a life insurance company and was opposed to investing in equities—Shafiroff was able to make the case that owning equity in a public company would fulfill his dream. Shafiroff proved to his client that the best way for him to become involved in the industry was through investing in a company that was trading on the stock market. By creating an investment vehicle that other financial advisors might never consider, Shafiroff served his client well. This story reveals how a creative salesperson can serve customers in ways that are beyond the imagination of mediocre ones. It also illustrates why Martin Shafiroff is viewed as a legend in the financial services industry.

The Treaty
of Toronto

Bob LaMonte

Sports Agent

★ ★ ★

B ob LaMonte founded *Professional Sports Representation Inc. (PSR) in 1979. At the time he was teaching history and coaching high school football in San Jose, California. PSR specializes in representing football coaches and top executives of National Football League (NFL) and National Collegiate Athletic Association (NCAA) teams. At present, the agency's NFL and NCAA roster includes 14 front office senior officials, 7 head coaches, 10 defensive and offensive coordinators, and 14 positional coaches, as well as 1 Major League Baseball player and 1 prominent ESPN broadcaster. Over the past 30-plus years, no other sports agency has represented more head coaches in the NFL. LaMonte has been recognized by* Sports Illustrated *as the most prominent coaches' agent in the United States.*

★ ★ ★

On a rainy day in late February 1983, right after school let out, I drove down Highway 101 to attend a 4 P.M. meeting at the Santa Clara Marriott with three Toronto Blue Jays executives to negotiate a contract for my client, Dave Stieb, the team's star pitcher. The team would be represented by vice president Paul Beeston, general manager Pat Gillick, and international director of scouting Wayne Morgan. They had agreed to come to Santa Clara because both Stieb and Morgan lived in Morgan Hill, which was 20 minutes south of the hotel. Plus, it would have been hard for me to travel due to my teaching schedule.

Stieb had been a punter at Oak Grove High School, where I taught. A natural athlete, he was a standout pitcher on the school's baseball squad. I had also coached Stieb's older brother, who had been a student in my history class. When Dave Stieb originally signed with the Blue Jays, I hadn't become an agent yet. Hence he was represented by somebody else.

Stieb had been playing for the Blue Jays since 1978, and in 1982, he posted a 17-14 record with a 3.25 earned run average. Toronto was an expansion team, and Stieb was its first starting pitcher to have a winning season. In 1982 he was named the American League Pitcher of the Year by *Sporting News* and was a three-time All Star pitcher. At age 24, he was in his prime, and I felt confident when I arrived at the Marriott. I had a wonderful client, and the Blue Jays wanted its promising pitcher to continue playing for the team.

The previous negotiations had been a disaster. Although Stieb was the team's number-one pitcher and the fans adored him, since his arrival in Toronto two of his sports agents had engaged in ongoing wars with the organization. They had made constant threats about taking Stieb to another team as soon as he became a free agent. In an arbitration case induced by his agent the previous year, he sought a bigger paycheck than was in his contract. Stieb lost and was paid only

$250,000, as stipulated in his contract, which ended after the 1983 season. The Toronto media had covered the continual disputes between Stieb and the franchise, and the hometown fans were eager to see an agreement reached. It was clear that if one wasn't, Stieb would have to play the last year of his contract and then be free to sign with another team. Toronto's management was thinking long-term and wanted to sign its star player to a multiyear contract.

I knew all this, and both sides understood that if Stieb signed for several years, his annual paycheck would need to be considerably more than $250,000. It was common knowledge in baseball circles that standout pitchers of his caliber were paid far more than the Blue Jays were paying him. If we didn't come to terms, we had the option of going to arbitration again. If that happened, it was probable that we'd lose and he'd have to finish out the final year of his contract. But after that, some other team would pick him up and he'd get a multimillion-dollar contract. My objective was to convince the team to think long-term vs. only the 1983 season.

Certainly the Blue Jays execs were apprehensive about sitting down with a history teacher, especially some guy who couldn't meet with them until late in the afternoon after school got out. I was sure they were thinking I must be some local yokel who didn't know diddly-squat about negotiating contracts.

I met with the three baseball executives in a small room off the hotel's main lobby. The meeting started off on a friendly note. There was some small talk about the rainy weather, which was unusual for California during that time of year, and one of them asked how a high school history teacher got into the sports agency business. I talked about my career, and all the while, they were trying to size me up. I had gone through this same routine before. I politely answered their questions. I felt the situation worked to my advantage because they knew nothing about me but I knew a lot about them.

I didn't want to disappoint anyone, so I played the part of the small-town school teacher and combined it with the disheveled look of detective Peter Falk in *Columbo*, a popular TV series in the 1970s.

I even had a trench coat I carried to the meeting and tossed it over my shoulder. Like Columbo, I used it as a prop to set the stage. I was nonchalant and came across as nonthreatening. It was my intention to catch them off guard, and I did.

Paul Beeston, the vice president, was the first to start the negotiations. "Let's talk business," he said, "and let's see what we can do so both sides can walk out of here happy."

"It's counterproductive to have a ballplayer with a chip on his shoulder," general manager Pat Gillick added.

"Gentlemen, I couldn't agree more," I replied. "I think we should approach this as a team effort. We are not adversaries. We want to do what's good for everyone. Let's work to what both sides can agree is a fair market value for the services of my client, and it will be a win-win for everyone."

"Well put," Beeston said.

I sensed that I put them in a positive frame of mind. I know agents who take a negative approach. They begin with the idea that it won't work, but I go in thinking that it's always going to work. I could have said to them, "Look, this is a deal that you haven't been able to get done before. Here's what we want—take it or leave it." I could have played hardball and said, "You can hold Dave to his contract for one year, that is, if we go into arbitration and you win. Or if we arbitrate and we win, he's gone and he'll be pitching for someone else come next spring." It had been a war between the team and Stieb's agents for years. I came in just the opposite. I said, "Hey, I'm a high school history teacher. I was Dave's friend and his brother's history teacher, and I think today, we probably should get something done."

Sure I was aware that it's very unnerving to an organization when they've been dealing with contentious, high-powered sports agents, and now I walk in as the kid's advisor. It was completely unprecedented. I understood that if I came across as a complete buffoon, they could have thought I didn't know what I was doing and it wouldn't be possible to deal with me. With this in mind, I knew I had to convince them I was a guy they could make a deal with.

For the next four hours we talked. While it was cordial, the meeting wasn't going anywhere. Then Beeston said, "Bob, there are three of us and one of you. I know the sides are unfair, but there are some things we should be talking about among ourselves but can't with you in the room. I hope you don't consider this impolite. . . ."

"Not at all," I told him, "because the way I see it, either the three of you will leave the room to talk to each other, or I can go out of the room and talk to myself."

They cracked up. If there was ever a turning point in a negotiation, that was it. It broke the ice and led to a breakthrough in the negotiations.

"And we thought there would be a problem negotiating with a high school teacher," Gillick said with a wide grin.

"You're okay," Beeston said to me.

In all business deals, you have to sell yourself to the other party. They liked me, and I liked them. We had established a rapport, and once that happens, reasonable people are generally able to compromise on the terms of an agreement that are satisfactory to both parties. Stieb's previous agents were confrontational. I never thought that's an effective way to negotiate with people. Besides, I really liked Paul Beeston, Pat Gillick, and Wayne Morgan—they were down-to-earth guys. And I felt comfortable with who I was. I was a school teacher and comfortable being a teacher. I didn't try to put on airs, nor was I ever arrogant. I wasn't there to impress anyone about how smart I was. Nor was I there to make unreasonable demands. I was there to do a job that required me to negotiate the best possible agreement for my client. These three gentlemen weren't adversaries. We were there to work together toward a goal that would benefit both parties. My strategy was to establish rapport with them; once that was achieved, coming up with the money for Stieb was the easy part. All professional baseball players' salaries are posted by the players union, so based on Stieb's past performance, I was able to come up with the numbers I wanted for him going forward. They knew he was worth my asking price and were agreeable to paying it.

By 10 o'clock that evening, we had agreed to all the terms, and they took out a 20-page boilerplate major league contract that I had reviewed prior to the meeting. We filled in all the blank spots pertaining to salary, time periods, incentives, and so on. We also inserted some handwritten addendums.

When we were through, I called Stieb. "Congratulations, Dave, you got yourself a $6.6 million, six-year contract with the Blue Jays. Come on down so you can sign the papers, and we'll all celebrate." He was shocked and ecstatic.

When the meeting was over, Beeston said, "We accomplished more in four hours with you, Bob, than we did in four years with Dave's previous representation."

The next morning, we all flew to Toronto and attended a major media conference at which the Blue Jays announced that a deal had been signed. It was a headline story in Toronto, all over the news. The media said that the fight between the Blue Jays and Stieb had officially ended. They hailed it as The Treaty of Toronto, and Stieb was thereafter known as "the Six-Million-Dollar Man."

★ Barry's and Bob's Comments ★

Bob LaMonte didn't try to put on airs and avoided confrontation. By being humble and sincere, he sold himself first. Once Beeston, Gillick, and Morgan were sold on LaMonte, the rest was an easy sell. It's really a simple, basic principle: people are more likely to do business with people they like than those they dislike. Unlike Stieb's previous representation, LaMonte was congenial and worked with the other side, not against them, and by doing so it was a win-win situation. Ideally, every sale should end up with both parties walking away delighted, thinking they made a wonderful deal. When this happens, long-term relationships sprout.

Your Reputation Is Your Most Valuable Asset

David L. Steward

Founder and Chairman, World Wide Technology

★ ★ ★

When David L. Steward founded World Wide Technology (WWT), specializing in advanced technology solutions focused on unified communications security wireless, and data center technologies, in St. Louis in 1990, he leveraged his entire life savings of $250,000 to fund the startup company. With annual revenues exceeding $4 billion, the privately held company is the nation's largest company with majority black ownership. Today WWT has more than 1,400 employees serving more than 3,000 manufacturers around the world. WWT's strategic partnerships include Cisco Systems, Dell, EMC, Hewlett-Packard, J.P. Morgan Chase, Sun Microsystems, and the U.S. Air

Force. The company is a systems integrator that provides innovative technology and supply-chain solutions to the commercial, governmental, and telecom sectors.

After graduating from Central Missouri State University with a business degree, Steward held various sales and marketing positions with Wagner Electric, Missouri Pacific Railroad, and Federal Express. In 1984 he started his own company, Transportation Business Specialists, and a sister company, Transport Administrative Services, that were forerunners to WWT.

Steward is one of St. Louis' top civic leaders. His past and current positions include serving as the chairman of the board of United Way of Greater St. Louis, president of the Greater St. Louis Area Council Boy Scouts of America, and president of the board of directors of Variety the Children's Charity of St. Louis. He received the National Urban League's Business Pioneer Award and the St. Louis County Economic Council Dr. William D. Phillips Technology Award, and he serves on the Board of Curators for the University of Missouri School System and numerous other committees and boards. He is the author of Doing Business by the Good Book *(2004), with a foreword written by former President George H. W. Bush. Steward was awarded Honorary Doctorates of Humane Letters by Harris Stowe State University and Lindenwood University.*

I n 1984 I was employed by Federal Express and named the company's Salesman of the Year. Founder and CEO Fred Smith presented me with a trophy, an ice bucket with my initials engraved on it. I looked inside the bucket and saw nothing. "Is this what I want in life?" I remember thinking—a pat on the back and "Atta boy, get back out there and go get 'em." That's when I started thinking seriously about starting my own business. My goal was to own a company that would serve its employees and customers.

My search for a business that I might acquire took me to St. Joseph, Missouri, a city with a population of about 75,000 that is 260 miles from St. Louis, on the border with Kansas. I went there to meet with Leo Moore, owner of Leo Moore Consulting Company. It was a small firm with 10 employees that audited shipping charges for companies to determine if they were overcharged by freight carriers. Leo and I had a few mutual friends dating back to my days when I was a salesman for the Missouri Pacific Railroad. We met while I was working for Federal Express, and from time to time, I'd stop in to chat with him when I was in St. Joe. We'd get together for lunch or dinner, and over a three-year period we got to know each other.

We hit it off because we shared the same values. Leo's word was his bond. He had integrity and was a man people could trust. Everyone who did business with Leo said that whatever he said he'd do, he would do. I was a top salesman for Missouri Pacific and FedEx because I built a reputation, like Leo, as someone who always did what he said he'd do. How did I become such a person? I was raised in Clinton, Missouri, a small town, and came from a poor family of ten. The focal point of my mother's life was the small church we belonged to—she taught Sunday school, served on committees, and practically every day of her life she spent time in church. I was blessed with two wonderful parents who had a set of values and beliefs that were the bedrock of who I am. They were wonderful role models.

When I entered the workforce as a sales rep, I always did what I'd said I'd do. It sounds so simple, and certainly everyone can adhere to this principle. Unfortunately, however, most people don't, and those who do stand above the crowd. I built a reputation by being such a person—every time, and over the years, I had a reputation as a man who never let people down. Rather than underperform, I overperformed. I always strived to deliver more than I promised.

I introduced Leo to several key managers with big corporations who, as a result, became his clients. Consequently, we had mutual friends, all of whom had good things to say about me. During one visit to St. Joe, Leo mentioned that he was 65 and was thinking about the day when he could sell his consulting firm. Leo lived in Kansas City, about 50 miles south of St. Joe, where he had other business interests. He felt it was time to slow down, and he was ready to sell his consulting firm at the right price.

For quite some time, I'd wanted to own my own business but didn't have the money to fund a company. I knew Leo's business and thought it could be the opportunity I was looking for.

"Leo, I don't have the money to buy your company," I told him, "but if you'll consider selling it to me with nothing down, I'll pay you out of future profits over the next three years."

"There is nobody I'd rather see own it," Leo said, "but I'll be taking a risk if you fail and aren't able to pay your debt to me. If so, the business won't have any value, and I won't be able to get anything for it."

"I understand," I said, "but I promise you that I'll work day and night to make it work, and if I didn't think I could do it, I wouldn't make you an offer."

"Let me think about it, Dave," he answered.

Leo did his due diligence by making a lot of calls to people I gave as referrals and mutual acquaintances of ours. Everyone told him that I had a lot of energy and didn't have a lazy bone in my body. They said that I knew the transportation business and was an excellent salesperson. Most importantly, they told him that if I said I'd pay him over a three-year period, they were confident that I would.

Certainly Leo talked to other people who said he would be making a horrendous mistake to sell to a black man who had never had a business of his own. And in truth, Leo had little background doing business with black people. Undoubtedly, it took a leap of faith for him to sell his company to me with no down payment. The biggest thing I had going for me was the fact that everyone who knew me spoke highly of me. Then, too, over the past three years, Leo and I had developed a strong relationship.

Leo sold me his business for $200,000 with nothing down. I couldn't afford to move the company to St. Louis, so for the next 12 months, I drove back and forth from St. Louis to St. Joe, putting in 80-hour weeks. St. Joe was in the middle of nowhere so it required me to spend many nights away from my family during my first year in business.

During that first year, I did what I did best, and that was selling our services. I opened new accounts with some of the biggest corporations in the U.S., companies such as General Motors, Ford, Chrysler, Abbott Laboratories, and Pfizer. Consequently, I was able to pay the full $200,000 to Leo at the end of the first year. Later I moved the company to St. Louis and changed its name to Transportation Business Specialists. The company was the forerunner to World Wide Technology.

In retrospect, selling myself to Leo Moore was the most important sale of my life. It was the sale that was responsible for launching my career as an independent businessperson.

⋆ Barry's and Bob's Comments ⋆

This story epitomizes how having a rapport with customers is the key to long-term relationships. Most importantly, it illustrates that your reputation is crucial to your success. Steward articulates how his family background advocated a life of strong religious values—principles that he learned as a youth that he applied his entire life. Steward never swayed from those beliefs, and they contributed significantly to his success throughout his business career. Steward has a sterling reputation in business and in his community—he is heralded as a man of high integrity. It was his long-term reputation that convinced Leo Moore to sell his business to him with no down payment. We can't overemphasize the value of a good reputation—over the course of time it is one's most valuable asset.

The Man Who Represents Dead Celebrities

Mark Roesler

CEO, CMG Worldwide

★ ★ ★

Mark Roesler is an intellectual property rights lawyer and entrepreneur. He is the founder, chairman, and CEO of CMG Worldwide, a marketing and management firm that acts as the business agent for more than 300 of the world's most recognizable celebrities, both dead and alive.

Born in Alexandria, Indiana, Roesler was his high school valedictorian in 1974 and enrolled at DePauw University. He financed his education working as a roofing contractor. He earned a joint J.D. and MBA degree at Indiana University. Upon finishing his formal education in 1981, he was hired as an intellectual property attorney by the Curtis Publishing Company, longtime publisher of

The Saturday Evening Post. *His job included licensing the copyrights to Norman Rockwell's work. Realizing that the families of deceased celebrities were unable to protect their famous relatives' intellectual property rights, Roesler formed Curtis Management Group in 1982, a division within the Curtis Publishing Company and the predecessor to his independent and privately owned company, CMG Worldwide Inc. (1986). That first year, he was hired by Elvis Presley's widow, Priscilla Presley, to represent her husband's estate. This marked the first of hundreds of estates of famous personalities Roesler has represented. In 1986, CMG Worldwide broke away from Curtis and became an independent company.*

Over the years Roesler has become known as an international authority in the area of intellectual property rights. Some of his notable legal successes include:

☆ *A 1988 legal battle with Major League Baseball, in which he won the right for retired players to wear their team uniforms while appearing to endorse products or services.*

☆ *A 1993 legal skirmish in which he represented Betty Shabazz, the widow of Malcolm X, against director Spike Lee. The court ruled that Shabazz controlled the rights to the "X" used in association with her late husband and should be paid a licensing fee by Lee.*

☆ *The 1997 O.J. Simpson civil trial, in which, as an expert witness, Roesler calculated Simpson's future net worth at $25 million. At the end of the trial, the families of Nicole Simpson and Ronald Goldman were awarded that exact sum.*

The long list of 300-plus celebrities represented by CMG Worldwide include James Dean, Marilyn Monroe, Ingrid Bergman, Marlon

Brando, Buddy Holly, Bette Davis, Babe Ruth, Lou Gehrig, Jesse Owens, Ella Fitzgerald, Billie Holiday, Malcolm X, Bettie Page, Jackie Robinson, Wilt Chamberlain, and Amelia Earhart. Living celebrity clients include Sophia Loren, Pamela Anderson, and Hugh Hefner.

★ ★ ★

In 1981, fresh out of law school and with my MBA, I got a job with Curtis Publishing Company, parent company of *The Saturday Evening Post.* I was hired to do legal work on the intellectual property rights involving most of Norman Rockwell's artwork, which had appeared on more than 300 magazine covers owned by the company.

Two years after I joined Curtis, I was having dinner in an Indianapolis restaurant with Greg Thomas, my good friend from law school. It was about ten at night when in the middle of our conversation, a thought hit me like a thunderbolt. "I have a great idea," I said to him. "I'm going to contact the family of James Dean tomorrow."

"Why would you want to do that?" Greg questioned.

"Elvis' widow, Priscilla, heard about the work I've been doing with the Norman Rockwell artwork," I said, "and she asked me to represent his estate. It's in litigation with Colonel Parker, Elvis' old agent. Graceland just opened, and they wanted to sell some high-quality Elvis merchandise. Along with other things, they're fighting with Parker over it." Thinking out loud, I continued, "I think there are ways I can help James Dean's family regarding intellectual properties."

"Go for it!" Greg said.

Growing up in Alexandria, Indiana (pop. 4,000), just 10 miles north of Fairmount (pop. 3,000), which was best known as James Dean's hometown, I knew all about the famed movie star. Of course we never met—we couldn't have. I was born on October 31, 1955, exactly one month after he was killed in a head-on automobile accident. At the time of his death at age 24, Dean was one of the movie industry's biggest stars. Although Jimmy was only in three movies, *East of Eden, Rebel Without a Cause,* and *Giant,* each is a classic. *Rebel Without a Cause* was released after his death, and it's the film that propelled his stardom to cult status. Because he died so young, his memory is forever frozen in time as a rebellious, misunderstood youth. Needless to say, he was a bigger-than-life hero to the local folk in our part of Indiana.

That Saturday morning, I drove to Fairmont, which is about 45 miles northeast of Indianapolis. I planned to talk to his Aunt Ortense and her son Marcus Winslow Jr. Jimmy was only 8 when his mother died. Winton Dean, whose work required him to travel extensively, didn't think he could properly raise his son, so he sent the young boy to live with his wife's brother, Marcus Winslow, and his family.

I went directly to the farmhouse where the Winslows lived. The two-story white frame house is a mile outside Fairmont. It had a big front porch shaded by mature oaks and sycamores. The farm had been owned by the Winslow family since 1830. I drove up a long gravel road and parked in front of the house.

I was greeted at the front door by Marcus Winslow Jr., who was Jimmy's kid stepbrother (although they were cousins, James and Marcus always referred to each other as brothers). Ten years younger, he worshipped his big brother. When we met, Marcus was 44. He and his family lived in a big farmhouse. They were accustomed to strangers knocking on their door. Over the years, thousands of devoted James Dean fans made their pilgrimage to the farmstead. The more aggressive ones took photos, asked questions, and walked the hollowed grounds where their beloved movie idol had once set foot.

"Good morning," I said to Marcus. "My name is Mark Roesler, and I'm an intellectual property lawyer with Curtis Publishing Company in Indianapolis."

Marcus graciously asked me to come in, and I briefly explained the nature of the work I did.

"You know what, Mark," he said, "I think we should include my mother in on the conversation. She lives in town just a mile away. Let's go to her house to talk."

He called her, and I heard him say, "Mom, there's a Mark Roesler here. He's a lawyer with *The Saturday Evening Post*. He wants to talk to us about Jimmy." There was a brief silence, and Marcus said, "Okay, we'll be there in five minutes."

An outgoing woman, Ortense was in her late 70s. She was warm and gracious. The Winslows were Quakers and had a simple lifestyle. They were unpretentious, down-to-earth people.

"I read that you were James' aunt and after his mother died, you and your husband raised him."

"Like he was our own son," she replied. "And Marcus Jr.," she said, glancing at her son. "Jimmy always referred to him as his little brother."

"We were closer than most brothers," Marcus added.

There were a few minutes of the usual small talk people make in getting to know one another. "Boy, it's been a long time since I last visited Fairmont," I said, "but the town doesn't seem to have changed over the years."

"What brought you to Fairmont?" she asked. "Did you come in for the James Dean Festival?"

"I grew up in Alexandria, ma'am," I said. "My dad delivered mail over there. When I was in high school, we used to drive to Fairmont. I don't recall their names, but there were a couple of diners on Main Street where we'd get a bite to eat."

They asked me if I knew so-and-so in Alexandria, and for the next few minutes we played the do-you-know game. It turned out there were a handful of mutual acquaintances. Then it was time to get down to business. I explained that I had been working on the intellectual rights regarding the Norman Rockwell artwork owned by Curtis Publishing and was just getting started doing work for the Elvis Presley estate.

"I understand what you are doing with the Norman Rockwell artwork," Ortense said, "but I'm not sure what you do for the Elvis Presley estate nor can I ascertain what it has to do with us."

"I believe that families of celebrities like Elvis Presley and Jimmy should be able to protect the name and likeness of their loved ones," I said, "and as you know, they aren't able to. In fact, I'm aware of a major marketing campaign in Japan called 'Heroes That Wore Levis' that centers on James Dean."

"I don't know about that one," Marcus said.

"There are so many of them we don't know about," Ortense added, "but that's the way it is with famous people after they die."

"Yes, ma'am, you're correct," I said, "but that doesn't make it right. Historically you and I have had the right to protect our name and likeness while we're alive because it's been considered a personal right as opposed to a property right. Now when I say 'personal right,' the law says that we can have a cause of action against somebody for an invasion of our privacy. But once we are dead, personal rights die with us and can't be protected."

"It doesn't seem right," Marcus said.

"I agree," I continued. "For example, let's say you had a grocery store and there was goodwill associated with it. Even though you died, the goodwill stayed with that grocery store because it's considered a tangible asset even though there's nothing tangible about goodwill— you can't see, hear, feel, taste, or smell it. Same is true with copyrights and trademarks. Even though they are all intangibles, they would stay with the grocery store. However, when a person dies, personal rights die with him or her."

"It sounds like a person doesn't have as many rights as a grocery store," Marcus said.

"That's true," I said, "and I don't think that's right."

"I don't either," Ortense said.

"But it's the law, isn't it? Marcus asked.

"When laws aren't right," I said, "we can try to change them."

"What's the likelihood of that?" she asked.

I explained to them that there was a legal foundation for what I planned to do. "There is a property right that your family should control," I pointed out, "and it should be you who decides when and how to profit from it."

They had modest lives, and I could see that money wasn't what motivated them. So instead of talking about the potential money they could receive, I stressed that they could control how the James Dean name and image would be used. "I will do my best to honor Jimmy's legacy," I assured them, "and do whatever I can to make the family proud. At the same time, we will prevent others from using his name and image in a way that you would not like."

"I can't tell you how many products that have Jimmy's image on them that we've come across," Ortense said.

"You wouldn't believe all the people who stop by to see us with Jimmy Dean products," Marcus said. "Are you saying that we can have control over all of that?"

"Yes, sir," I said. "I've been working for a year on the Norman Rockwell artwork, and now I'm representing the Elvis Presley estate, which is engaged in a lawsuit with Colonel Parker. With the combination of these two experiences, I think that from both a legal and intellectual property standpoint, we are proceeding down a path that nobody has been down before. Based on my experience, I feel we are moving in a direction that is both fair and logical. I am confident that we have a legal foundation on which to stand and will prevail."

"Are you saying you want to change the existing law?" Marcus asked.

"Yes, it is possible that we could help change some of the various laws that are state statutes. I believe that as we move down the road, we will prevail in litigation."

After about an hour, Ortense said, "You've given us a lot to think about, Mark."

"Yes, I want you to think it over. And if it's okay with both of you, I'd like to come back in a couple of weeks."

Two weeks later, it was agreed that I would represent the family's interest in the James Dean estate.

We have been very successful in protecting the James Dean intellectual property rights. We have generated tens of millions of dollars in royalties for the family coming from billions of dollars of sales.

As a footnote, in 1991, out of the clear blue sky, Warner Bros., the company that produced Dean's three movies, sued us for $90 million under the RICO Act that Congress used to go after the Mafia. They filed the case in California in Federal Court. I was personally sued under RICO, with the suit claiming that, among other things, I committed wire and mail fraud. After 15 months the case went to trial. Meanwhile we were spending $250,000 a month in legal fees. A main issue was that Dean signed a standard Screen Actors Guild (SAG) contract that was written during the '30s to '50s era that didn't contemplate the intellectual property rights of celebrities, which weren't explored until the 1980s. In a two-week trial, we won every single issue on the case. The judge ruled that Warner Bros. had absolutely no rights by virtue of their standard SAG contracts. The court also ruled that Warner Bros. would not be given any right to use any James Dean image they had for anything outside the movies themselves. We turned around and countersued Warner Bros. for $100 million for malicious prosecution and quickly settled for a significant sum of money. Our legal skirmish with Warner Bros. is now considered one of the landmark cases in the entertainment industry because it established that the studios owned none of those intellectual property rights. Had we lost the case, CMG Worldwide would not be in business today.

☆ Barry's and Bob's Comments ☆

When Mark Roesler met with the Winslow family for the first time, he didn't have a secretary call them to set up a meeting. Nor did he call to arrange a meeting at his office in Indianapolis. That might have been the approach used by others— some would have thought that walking through the lobby and offices of *The Saturday Evening Post* would have been impressive to small-town Indiana folk. And, as all Hoosier basketball fans know, the home court team has a six-point advantage. Those thoughts never entered Roesler's mind. Instead, he got in his car and drove to Fairmont on a Saturday morning and dropped in to introduce himself. Instead of trying to come across as a high-powered attorney, he was humble and sincere. Having grown up in Alexandria, just ten miles away, Roesler let Marcus and Ortense Winslow know that he was one of them—somebody whom they could trust to do what he said he'd do.

Note, too, that Roesler was familiar with the kind of people the Winslows were—he understood their beliefs and values. He knew that they were more interested in protecting the good name of their beloved Jimmy Dean than the money that could potentially be made by owning the intellectual rights. This is a cardinal rule in selling any product or service: Always take the time to find out what the other person wants—and focus on it, rather than focusing on what you want to sell him!

When Selling Abroad, Be Sure to Understand the Culture

L. Kevin Kelly

CEO, Heidrick & Struggles

★ ★ ★

Kevin Kelly is the CEO of Heidrick & Struggles, an international global leadership advisory firm headquartered in Chicago. Founded in 1953, the company is the world's premier executive search consulting firm and has more than 60 offices in 35 countries around the world. With its international presence, Heidrick & Struggles has the capacity to serve its clients wherever they are located within the framework of a responsive international partnership. The firm has placed top executives at such firms as Citigroup, Google, Yahoo! and Merck. A Wall Street Journal survey in 2000 ranked Heidrick & Struggles the best executive search firm in the world in terms of quality of candidates, *reputation, and value of services among senior-level decision makers in corporate America.*

Kelly received his bachelor's degree from George Mason University and an MBA from Duke University's Fuqua School of Business and has been in the search industry since 1993. He joined Heidrick & Struggles' Tokyo office in 1997, served as regional managing partner of Asia Pacific and then Europe, the Middle East, and Africa (2001– 2006), and was named chief executive officer in 2006.

He is the author of CEO: The Low Down of the Top Job *and* Leading in Turbulent Times.

★ ★ ★

When I went to work at the firm's Tokyo office in 1997, we didn't have any Japanese clients, although we did have some foreign companies that had offices there. I was sent there to open new accounts with domestic companies. Selling in Japan, a country with a much different culture than ours, was challenging. This was especially true for a search firm because in Japan everything is grown from within. Japanese companies rarely hire anyone from a direct competitor. For instance, you'd rarely see Toyota hire someone from Nissan. So I knew from the start that selling a search firm's services wasn't going to be what you'd call a walk in the park. However, we were determined to get into the market because we were certain that our services would benefit Japanese-based companies.

I did my homework and ascertained that the Long Term Credit Bank was a good prospect for our services. It was a successful Japanese domestic-based bank with branches across the globe, and it was strong in Japan. However, due to cultural differences, it had difficulties attracting foreigners to come to Japan. And as a consequence, its main source for new managers came from Japanese nonbanking companies. It wasn't as if it had never tried to attract foreigners to come to work in

Japan. It did, but that never worked, and in the process the bank had wasted a lot of money. Knowing that Long Term Credit Bank was in the midst of developing new products to sell globally, I believed it needed to recruit senior foreign executives in the financial services business. These would be the people with the expertise to develop competitive financial products that could go head-on with products developed by western companies.

It would have been helpful to have a Japanese client make a formal introduction for me, but unfortunately I didn't have one. So I made a cold telephone call to one of the bank's senior people. I got through to his secretary, and the conversation ended with my telling her, "I would like to send a brochure to you that will explain the services that Heidrick & Struggles provides," and her agreement to pass it along to her boss. Prior to my phone call, neither she nor her boss had ever heard of Heidrick & Struggles. The brochure, printed in Japanese, highlighted the services we provided, some of our high-profile clientele, and our global presence.

I called a week or so later and set up a meeting to visit the bank. A secretary took me to a room where three men were seated at a small conference table. I introduced myself and felt good about the fact that they were able to pronounce Heidrick & Struggles correctly. That's always a hurdle, and I was glad it was behind me.

It was obvious that one of the men was the senior person, at the managing director level. I knew that it was proper etiquette in Japan to address my remarks mainly to him. At the same time, I was careful to acknowledge the other two men, who were at the vice president level, but always aware of being deferential and respectful to the most senior person in the room.

I explained the history of our firm, and they couldn't have been more polite. They listened intently. The problem, however, was that they only listened. It was a one-way conversation, and I was the only person talking. I have always believed that it's better for a salesperson to avoid dominating the conversation. Selling is just as much about listening as it is about talking—in fact, it may be more about listening than talking! While I thoroughly appreciated their attentiveness, their silence made it impossible to gather any feedback from them.

I kept waiting for a comment such as, "OK, that sounds interesting," or "I see what your company does." I would have even liked to hear a simple, "OK." But they remained silent.

The meeting lasted about 40 minutes. I told them what they needed to know about our firm, explained our capabilities, and told them why I thought we could help them by bringing in fresh talent that would put them in a more competitive position. All the time I kept asking questions such as, "Do you have any questions?" and "Is there anything I haven't explained that you would like to know?" Each time I tried to engage them in the conversation, I got nowhere. They were completely stoic—faces blank and showing no sign of interest. I recalled once seeing a comedian who told jokes while the audience just sat there and nobody laughed. I remember the compassion I felt for that performer. That was how I was feeling during my presentation. Just as the comedian knew he was bombing when nobody laughed at his jokes, I knew I was bombing. Just the same, I continued on with my presentation, having an empty feeling that I was wasting my time and had no chance of making a sale.

When my presentation was over, none of them had much to say. They just stood up, politely shook my hand, and thanked me. "Wow, what a complete waste of time," I thought to myself. "That was a huge bomb. I don't know if I'll ever completely recover from it." As a salesperson, you know when you have a good pitch and a bad one. You feel it when you walk out of there. I wanted to write it off as a bad experience and tried not to dwell on it. I just wanted to wipe it out of my mind.

You can imagine my shock when I received a call 2½ months later from the bank and was told, "We would like you to come back to discover more about how we can have a partnership with your firm."

"Wow," I remember thinking. "These guys actually called back." I couldn't figure it out. I had no idea what they could have been thinking during those 2½ months.

We set a date to meet, and this time I brought along a Japanese colleague to accompany me. Although I had been studying Japanese, I was by no means fluent so I didn't want to get into any negotiations where I'd run into problems.

At the first meeting I presented a general explanation about Heidrick & Struggles. The second meeting was different because this time they had prepared questions to ask me. This time they asked everything from how we could help them to how our fee structure worked.

I never knew for sure what happened between my first and second presentations that influenced their decision to invite me back again. Although I didn't give them any referrals of Japanese companies in Japan where we had placed someone, I did give them the names of some Japanese entities that did business with us overseas. I'm sure they must have done some checking, but I can't swear to it.

About nine months after my initial call with the bank, we placed a foreign executive whom they hired as a management director in charge of structured products.

★ Barry's and Bob's Comments ★

Kevin Kelly points out that an obvious lesson from this sale is that patience is a virtue. He emphasizes that it is important to understand how to sell in another country because the differences in cultures are likely to influence the outcome of the sale. Another lesson that Kelly's story teaches is that you should use caution when prejudging a prospect's reaction to your sales presentation. In Kelly's case, he concluded that the lack of animation and positive response from the three bank executives was a definite sign of disinterest. Obviously this was not the case. But then, we've all come across an overly zealous prospect who appeared to be a "sure sale" but never closed the sale. We believe that this story has a valuable lesson. Be careful not to size up a prospect and assume that his silence or, for that matter, his enthusiasm is a sure sign of his intentions. After all, selling and life itself are full of surprises.

The Biggest Sale
That Almost Didn't
Happen

Dave Liniger

Co-Founder and Chairman of the Board, RE/MAX

★ ★ ★

Dave Liniger co-founded RE/MAX, a global real estate network of franchisee-owned and -operated offices. Starting in Denver with a single office, Liniger and his wife, Gail, started the company in 1973. Today RE/MAX has about 90,000 affiliated independent sales professionals in more than 80 countries. There are more than 70 regional subfranchisors in the RE/MAX network, most of them independent of RE/MAX LLC, and varying in size from a metropolitan area to an entire country.

Dave and Gail's motivation to start the company was their dissatisfaction with how the real estate business was conducted at the time. Most real estate offices used the commission-split system, requiring sales professionals to forfeit half of their earnings to their brokers; in return they were provided a desk and other services. Consequently, the top producers contributed the most to the operation's overhead, paying a disproportionate share in comparison to the low-producing agents, who typically worked part time and lacked professionalism. With RE/MAX, in exchange for sharing office overhead and paying a management fee, associates receive a higher commission, along with business-building benefits and services.

The Linigers' business plan worked. Each year since 1997, the company's slogan has been true—nobody in the world sells more real estate than RE/MAX. The network's red, white, and blue hot air balloon logo is known around the world. The name RE/MAX was coined from the words "real estate" and "maximum," referencing a business model that provides maximum commissions.

Liniger has been inducted into the Council of Real Estate Brokerage Managers Hall of Leaders and the Real Estate Buyer's Agent Council Hall of Fame, and he has received the Council of Residential Specialists Special Achievement Award. He is a member of the International Franchise Hall of Fame. In 2010 he was included in Bloomberg BusinessWeek's profiles of the "50 Most Powerful People in Real Estate." He has been featured in Entrepreneur, Forbes, Fortune, Inc. magazine, Success, and other leading publications and media outlets around the world.

Along with his wife, Liniger co-founded The Wildlife Experience, a conservation center located just south of Denver that has a 14-acre, 111,000-square-foot venue. He also owns the acclaimed Sanctuary Golf Course, near Sedalia, Colorado, which is primarily devoted to charity golf tournaments. It has raised more than $50 million for hundreds of organizations since opening in 1997.

★ ★ ★

RE/MAX had only been selling franchises for four years when I received a phone call from Sid Syvertson, who, with his partner, Steve Hazelton, had one of the largest real estate firms in the U.S. Their company, Spring Realty, had about 1,000 agents with offices throughout Los Angeles.

Sid called to tell me that he was interested in buying a RE/MAX franchise. I said to him, "Sid, you've got a big company, and I have fewer than 100 agents in California. You're ten times our size, and we're spread all over the state, not just in one market, where you have a dominant position. I'm not sure I understand why you would consider a RE/MAX franchise."

"My plan is to convert all of my offices and agents from the commission-split system to the RE/MAX format," he replied, "and we'll have between 15 to 20 franchises."

I didn't take him seriously, figuring he was trying to do some competitive intelligence to find out what we did in order to compete with us. "Fine, Sid," I told him, "I'll send you some information and call me back if you're interested." I didn't bother to pursue it because I thought it was an absolute nonsensical lead that would go nowhere.

I sent the information to him, and a week later he called again. "I like what I read, and we are interested," Sid said.

I was thinking to myself that it was just a joke, and I was making a fool of myself. Again I put him off, telling him how busy I was, and I said, "I'll get back to you, Sid," thinking he had ulterior motives.

He was persistent and called again. "I really want to come to Denver to see you, Dave," he told me.

"Look, Sid, we're headed to Toronto for our summer leadership conference that's attended by all of our franchisees," I said. "Why don't you fly up, and you and your partner will be my guest? You can take a look around for two or three days and you'll have an opportunity to talk to a couple hundred of my brokers from the United States and Canada. If you're still interested, you can give me a call."

At this point, I wanted him to see the power of RE/MAX. Sid would be able to see that my people were really enthused about what we did. I figured it couldn't hurt to have them at this meeting. They came, and I was busy every minute, so other than being able to shake hands with them and say hello, I didn't spend time with them. I thought this would be the end of it and I'd never hear from Sid again.

A few weeks later, my secretary walked into my office. "There's a Sid Syvertson from Spring Realty in the reception area. Mr. Syvertson said that he would like to see you right now."

I cordially greeted him and said, "Sid, it's so nice to see you. Did you enjoy our convention?"

"I did," he answered.

"Sid, what can I do for you?"

He didn't say a word. Instead he took out a certified check for a quarter of a million dollars from his briefcase and slid it across the table. He looked at me and said, "Dave, I don't want to just buy franchises. I want to buy the California region."

I was in total shock. A quarter of a million dollars was a huge amount of money to our company at that time. I knew that if he bought the region, he'd have to terminate a lot of his agents, but we'd be way ahead because we'd end up with 200 of Spring Realty's top producers, which would be double the number we already had.

I looked at him in amazement and said, "Sid, I don't understand this. We haven't been successful in converting even small real estate offices that have 10 or 15 agents, and you're talking about converting the biggest thing in our history. Why in the world would you want to do that?"

"Dave, would you mind if I used your phone and put it on speaker?" he asked. "I want to make three calls and I want you to hear the conversations."

"OK," I replied, curious about what he was going to do.

With the speakerphone on, he called Rich Port, who owned Rich Port, Realtor, a firm about the same size as his that was the biggest in the Chicago area. Syvertson and Port were members of an elite group of realtors known as "the Dozen" who met on a regular basis to brainstorm. I knew the group was anti-RE/MAX. Sid got right to the point and asked Port, "Tell me about this RE/MAX franchise network. I know they've been in the Chicago area for a while, but they're not a factor in the California real estate market."

"Oh, it's an amazing thing," Port responded. "RE/MAX came here about five years ago, and we laughed. The first year they opened a couple of franchises. The next year they opened four or five more, and we were thinking, 'You know, they're just like another Century 21 or ERA. But by gosh, in the last year or so, they've become number one in the market, and I'm losing dozens of my top producers to them. I don't know how to compete."

They chatted for a while, and when Syvertson hung up, he dialed a big broker in Atlanta and had the same conversation. "They came in and opened a couple of offices. We didn't think anything of it. A couple of years later, they opened another ten, and then all of a sudden, after about five years, they're number one in Greater Atlanta, and I'm losing all my top producers to them."

His last call was to Sven Nylund, senior vice president of Van Schaack & Company, a major competitor in Denver. I knew Sven, who is one of the finest men you'll ever meet. After some small talk, Syvertson asked, "What can you tell me about RE/MAX?"

"We had this young kid," Nylund replied, "Dave Liniger, who was about 25 years old when he came up here from Phoenix. Liniger kept talking to all of our managers and me about why we didn't convert to this commission concept. He said it works like a co-op and is modeled after a group of doctors or lawyers who share the expenses of running the business, pay their personal expenses, and keep the vast majority of their income for themselves. He said Van Schaack should do it and go national and even international with it. We didn't think it had any merit. Liniger said that we laughed at him, so he went out and did it on his own. He struggled and in the beginning didn't do much business. He experienced all the problems that startups have, but lo and behold, five years later, he was off and running. We had never lost an agent to him before, and all of a sudden, he had 300-plus agents and was number one in the Denver market. Soon we were losing dozens and dozens of our top producers, who left us and joined his firm. We don't know how to compete with him."

Nylund paused and asked, "Why do you ask, Sid?"

"I'm negotiating with Dave to buy the California rights. I'm going to convert my offices to it," Syvertson said. "I think it's the future of the real estate industry. It seems to work, and the agents are in love with the concept. I know it will mean that in order for us to keep our top people, we'll have to pay them a lot more than we do now. It seems to be a paradigm shift."

"If I were you, I'd do it," Nylund said.

Sid put down the phone, and I said, "Do you realize that you'll have to fire 800 of your 1,000 agents when we start this conversation?"

"I know it," he said. "They're friends, and my partner and I like all of these people. It will be difficult." He looked at me and added, "We've built a little empire, but we realize that the future of this business will be the top producers. And if that means taking a step or two backward to go forward again, that's what we'll do. I want to be part of this."

It was a gutsy call for Syvertson. However, over the next 20 years or so, he built a huge empire with hundreds of offices and a large staff. He was 20 years or so older than I, and in 2007, our organization repurchased his company for an amount in excess of $100 million. Evidently, he made the right move that turned out to be a very good investment. Sid and I became best friends. Unfortunately, about a year after we bought him out, he passed away.

Sid was one of my biggest supporters, and the conversion of his firm gave our company tremendous credibility. It made the entire real estate industry stand up and take notice. He was definitely a major catalyst that contributed to our success over the next several years.

★ Barry's and Bob's Comments ★

As every salesperson is taught early on in his career, never prejudge a prospect. When this lesson is taught, for the most part it applies to misjudging a small prospect that appears unable to afford your product or service. For instance, a salesperson in a retail store might think a person dressed in rags doesn't have the money to spend on an expensive item like a new car or high-priced furniture. Hence the prospect is given the cold shoulder. As every experienced retailer knows, you should never predetermine who will be a big sale or who won't.

Liniger's reaction was the opposite. He thought that a highly successful prospect like Sid Syvertson wasn't really interested in his marketing concept but instead wanted to learn about his company to pick up a few pointers on how to compete against him. As he points out, "The lesson I learned was to be open-minded. I talked to hundreds of conversions, and when one of them came along that would do it, I should not have given up, especially when a big prospect came begging to buy. It taught me to never stop working all the angles of my market. If you do, you'll never get the big hit that I got—the one that really put us on the map."

Open-Mindedness Pays Off

Deborah Dunsire, M.D.
President and CEO, Millennium: The Takeda Oncology Company

★ ★ ★

Deborah Dunsire was named president and CEO of Millennium Pharmaceuticals Inc. in July 2005. Previously Dr. Dunsire was with Novartis Pharmaceuticals Corporation and its predecessor company Sandoz, which she joined in 1988 in a clinical research capacity. She moved to managing the specialty products division in South Africa, then to the headquarters in Basel, Switzerland, and later to the United States, where she served as vice president of Novartis' Oncology Business Unit. In 2000 she became head of North American Oncology Operations. In this capacity, Dr. Dunsire spearheaded six new product/indication launches, including Gleevec, the first targeted therapy for *chronic myeloid leukemia (CML). Gleevec was hailed as a major breakthrough medicine for treating a rare form of cancer with a very low patient survival rate. Dr. Dunsire also managed the merger and growth of the company's Sandoz and Ciba oncology businesses.*

As president and CEO of Millennium, Dunsire headed a team that built the business into a fast-growing biotech company with a leading therapy, VELCADE®, approved for treating multiple myeloma and previously approved for treating mantle cell lymphoma, and with a robust pipeline of cancer and inflammation product candidates. In an unexpected turn of events, she and her team negotiated the successful acquisition of the company by Takeda Pharmaceutical Company, a global industry leader. Takeda is the largest pharmaceutical company in Japan and one of the top 20 pharmaceutical companies worldwide.

Dr. Dunsire earned her medical degree at the University of the Witwatersrand in Johannesburg, South Africa, and worked as a partner in a general practice in Johannesburg from 1986–88. She speaks fluent English, German, and Afrikaans, is proficient in French, and is currently working on her Japanese.

T wo years prior to my arrival at Millennium, the company launched VELCADE®, a first-in-class drug that was the first treatment for relapsed multiple myeloma, a rare blood disease, to be approved by the FDA in more than a decade. When I became CEO in 2005, I succeeded Mark Levin, who had founded the company in 1993. Millennium's biggest asset was its people, particularly its team of dedicated and highly skilled scientists, and in this business, if you don't get the science right, you don't get anything right. VELCADE was a breakthrough drug, and I realized that in order for it, or for that matter the company itself, to reach its full potential we would have to strengthen the commercial side of the business to raise it to the same level of sophistication as our scientific organization. This would require shifting the balance of resources from the R&D side to the commercial side.

At the time, I felt our sales force's approach was too academic. Sales representatives distributed scientific literature to extremely busy physicians who were overwhelmed by too much technical information. Consequently, the physicians had difficulty absorbing so much material. In time we were able to make VELCADE a successful brand, and Millennium began to experience rapid growth in the marketplace, achieving blockbuster status in 2008 with worldwide sales in excess of $1 billion. Concurrently, we achieved clinical milestones with other medicines in the Millennium pipeline. The company was becoming well-positioned in the marketplace and progressing at a healthy pace. As a result of this compounding success, we attracted the attention of Takeda Pharmaceutical Company of Japan, whose leaders viewed Millennium as a possible drug development partner.

Although the initial talks between our two companies focused primarily on how Millennium and Takeda might collaborate on drug development opportunities, it was during those preliminary discussions that Takeda began to think beyond partnering with us and began its own internal discussions about taking this potential partnership in a different direction. A team of Millennium's cross-functional leadership—from discovery research to commercialization, from executive to finance and business development—participated in the preparation. During previous visits, the Takeda scientific leaders were very interested in seeing our people in their own work environment. What they saw was a highly competent and strongly motivated workforce—individuals who talked with passion about what they do and who articulated why their work was important and where they were going with it.

As the Takeda executives discovered, we were entrepreneurs who didn't shy away from taking well-calculated business risks with high potential for reward. They observed people who care about the work and take pride in doing it right, with the ultimate goal of creating medicines that benefit patients. They were able to see that our organization was not burdened with bureaucracy. We had the capacity to respond quickly to get things done.

In early January 2008, Anna Protopapas, our head of business development, and I attended JP Morgan's annual health-care conference in San Francisco. That evening we joined Yasu Hasegawa, the president of Takeda, and two of his colleagues. During dinner, Hasegawa-san said, "We've talked to you for a while about the many different structures of the deal. We discussed research, collaboration, partnership, product, and having the opportunity to get to know your company, and we believe Millennium is exactly what Takeda needs in order to catalyze our ability to become an oncology leader."

Choosing his words carefully, he said, "We looked at companies that could expand our knowledge in a certain area, could expand our geographic presence, but most important for us to consider is the values fit and the integrity of the company. When we evaluate a merger candidate, we place a high emphasis on the company's integrity and the fit of our values, and if there is any question about it, we will pass on it."

He paused briefly and said, "Dr. Dunsire, we would like to make an offer for your company."

"We are a small company," I replied, "and we have a lot we want to get done. I want you to know that being acquired is not the strategy we have in mind for our company. But we will do our fiduciary duty and evaluate your initial offer to determine its value to our shareholders."

He listened intently and nodded to indicate his consent.

"The same people who will be involved in the diligence are the ones who are building our company," I emphasized, "so we can't take a long time and drag our feet. We don't want to be distracted. If the acquisition doesn't happen, we want to make sure that we don't take our eye off the ball and have our business suffer."

"I understand," he said politely.

"How quickly do you think Takeda can get through the initial diligence?" I asked.

"About one month," he replied.

Hasegawa-san was true to his word. They moved incredibly fast.

As CEO and director of a publicly owned company, I had a fiduciary responsibility to evaluate in good faith what was best for our shareholders, even if it was not what I personally desired. At the time, Millennium was prospering and growing, so being acquired was not part of our strategic plan. Just the same, the management team and board fulfilled our duties and evaluated the unexpected offer. We assessed the value we saw within the company from our product, pipeline, and research capabilities, which could continue to progress molecules for sustainable growth into the future. And we could see that if the company were fully valued, our shareholders would receive a guaranteed return today rather than waiting for a potential payoff in the future, which was inherently riskier. The acquiring company would be able to build value for itself, too. Millennium would allow Takeda to achieve critical mass in oncology and a stronger U.S. presence much more quickly than through organic growth.

The Millennium team was determined to tell our entire story, the vision for our future and the substance of why we believed we could achieve it. Only then could Takeda develop a clear idea how we might bring value to the venerable 200-plus-year-old, highly successful company. Yes, we had VELCADE, a new blockbuster product on the market with even more growth potential. But we were much more than a one-product pharmaceutical company. We had a pipeline of other medicines and a team of committed scientists. We believed that we had the capability to build value well beyond what appeared on the surface.

We went into hyperdrive to prepare for Takeda's diligence review. I assembled my team, which included Anna Protopapas, Kyle Kuvalanka, head of investor relations, and Lisa Adler, head of communications, along with the leaders of our scientific and medical functions—Joe Bolen, our chief scientific officer, Nancy Simonian, our chief medical officer, Pete Smith, the leader of our preclinical evaluation, and Christophe Bianchi, who drove the commercial success. Central to our preparations was Marsha Fanucci, our chief financial officer and head of corporate strategy, our general counsel, Laurie Keating, and head of human resources Steve Gansler; ably assisted by our outside counsel, Wilmer Hale, and Goldman Sachs, our investment banking firm. All of us prepared and tested our thinking under the guidance of our board of directors.

When it became apparent that Takeda was going to make an offer for our company rather than consider us as a development partner, we had extensive communications with its negotiation team and with Hasegawa-san prior to an actual meeting. Before initiating the formal diligence review, a "summit" meeting was set up to allow the Millennium and Takeda leadership teams to talk through all the sources of current and future value in Millennium. Then, to allow Takeda to perform its due diligence and verify what we had said and establish its own assessment, we submitted all relevant documents for their scrutiny by way of an electronic "room." It was fortunate that during our earlier discussions the scientific leaders from Takeda had toured our headquarters in Cambridge, Massachusetts, because, once acquisition discussions began, it was imperative that only a very small group of leaders were involved so the whole organization did not become concerned and distracted, speculating about the potential outcomes. All our meetings were held far away from the company at a newly opened local hotel—the Liberty Hotel (formerly a penitentiary!).

Karen Ferrante, M.D., who was the number-two person in our clinical development group, listened pensively to our presentation. As we walked out of one of the meetings with our Takeda visitors, Karen said to me, "When I listened to who we are and what we are capable of achieving, I thought to myself, *we are just priceless.*"

During this period we got to know the Takeda people and we liked what we saw. Evidently they liked what they saw too. After some negotiating, they acquired Millennium for $8.8 billion, which, at that time, was the largest pharmaceutical-biotechnology acquisition made by a Japanese pharmaceutical company and the second largest acquisition of an American company by a Japanese company. Our shareholders received a 53 percent premium over the stock price of the last trading day prior to the announcement of the deal on April 10, 2008.

Prior to the public announcement, only a tight team working on the diligence and negotiations knew about Takeda's interest in Millennium. As soon as we issued our press release, the media, including the *Wall Street Journal,* the *New York Times,* the *Boston Globe,* Dow Jones, the Associated Press, Reuters, Bloomberg, and CNBC, covered the story extensively. Thus many of our people heard about the acquisition before getting to work that morning. That same day we pulled together an ad hoc employee meeting. All of our Cambridge-based employees, some 850–900 people, assembled at a town hall meeting in a hotel ballroom.

As CEO, it was my job to tell them who Takeda was, why it was interested in Millennium, and why it would be a good thing for Millennium to become a part of Takeda. I felt comfortable talking to them because I had gotten to know the Takeda management team and was convinced that they were committed to keeping our talented people and engaging them to build Takeda's oncology leadership. Yasu Hasegawa had emphasized to me how Takeda had the same mission and shared our same values. "Dr. Dunsire, it is your job as the president of Millennium to make sure the people stay," he said to me. "We know that you need to keep your culture and foster it because it's part of the reason why people stay here."

Knowing how he valued the people at Millennium, I felt that there were few CEOs facing what I was facing—telling people that their company had new ownership—who would have had the privilege I had of joining with that acquisition announcement the plans of future growth and support for our strategy and culture. I had to put my reputation with our employees on the line as I spoke passionately about this deal, which while completely unexpected gave us the opportunity to become a global leader in oncology and to invest far more in our pipeline than we could as an independent entity. I had to ask them to trust me and their management team. I was willing to do that. I learned through our interactions to trust Yasu Hasegawa as the president of the company he represented and to take him at his word. I knew that they were honorable people of the highest integrity. This made it easy for me to stand up in front of all of our people and ask them to support the transaction.

I started by letting them know about Takeda. "This is a company that has been around for 230 years," I said. "They were founded by a single family and now Kunio Takeda, who is the seventh generation of family members to run the company, is chairman. Takeda has been around for a long time—and like Millennium, it is a company that takes a long-term view. It isn't driven quarter to quarter. This is a company that, like Millennium, is committed to patients and wants to be a leader in contributing to the cure of cancer. Ladies and gentlemen, I am pleased to say that we share the same values."

After I told them about Takeda's impressive track record as Japan's premier pharmaceutical company, I talked to them about how they personally would benefit from the merger. "Takeda is committed to make this merger succeed," I continued. "This is a company that values its human resources as its most precious asset."

I talked to them about how I had gotten to know Yasu Hasegawa. I explained how he was sensitive to how they might react. "Let me share with you a conversation I had with Mr. Hasegawa. 'Perhaps your people will be concerned about being acquired by a Japanese company,' he said. 'They might even think that our words aren't true about our wanting you to run this business. So we will have incentives to let them know that we want them to run the business.'"

I talked about how Hasegawa-san assured me that all Millennium senior management would remain here. "Takeda is prepared to back its commitment up," I said, "with the assurance that all employees in good standing will be invited to stay, and to encourage them to do so, they will be given incentives. Mr. Hasegawa pledged to me that Takeda shares our vision, and the company is prepared to back it up by putting a retention package in place for every employee in good standing to be sure we keep the capabilities that Takeda desires. It will include some modest financial incentives to stay for one year. Takeda is doing this so that you will have the opportunity to take the time to get to know them and then make an informed decision on whether you want to continue working here or go elsewhere."

I concluded by saying, "I am confident that with Takeda, we will have greater resources to invest in research and development, and consequently our pipeline will grow."

Following my speech, we had a Q&A, and when the meeting ended, there was a round of enthusiastic applause that indicated their approval.

✰ Barry's and Bob's Comments ✰

In this story, Dr. Dunsire had to make two sales. Her first was to Takeda. By doing her homework, she understood the cultural background of Takeda. She knew it was interested in long-term results and believed that a company's most important asset is a dedicated work force. Dr. Dunsire understood that this coincided with Millennium's culture. She emphasized these strengths and how because of this, Takeda was able to value Millennium 43 percent higher than its then trading price.

Then at the town hall meeting, Dr. Dunsire had to convince Millennium's workforce to get on board. Wisely, she announced what was most important to them. First, they should not fear working for a Japanese parent company because the two companies shared a similar culture of integrity and a vision for helping patients. Second, she emphasized how Takeda valued people as the company's most valuable asset. Third, Dr. Dunsire assured them that Takeda's management team didn't just "talk the talk," they "walked the walk." This point was made clear when she explained the retention package to be given to all employees in good standing who stayed on for one year.

Dr. Dunsire said that a lesson to be learned from her story is that you should not be committed to succeed by strictly adhering to only one path. "Things happen that may require you to figure out another way," she emphasized. "You don't want to miss opportunities because they seem completely different than what you had in mind. By being open-minded, you can learn an awful lot. Being too comfortable only in your own way is a dangerous trait."

Another lesson she learned is that vast differences in culture, language, background, and geography are eclipsed when common goals and values are shared and respect is mutually offered. She emphasized the importance of people taking time to listen carefully to one another so they can fully understand the results they want to achieve and share the same motivations.

We concur. Successful people are flexible and open-minded about unexpected opportunities. Never wear blinders. One should recognize that there are many roads to take, and as the idiom tells us, "All roads lead to Rome." Dunsire points out that this is particularly good advice to keep in mind when working with people from different cultures.

A Captive Audience

Alan Levy

Founder, CEO, Cinchcast Inc.

★ ★ ★

Alan Levy is the chairman and CEO of Cinchcast Inc., a voice-based online communications company head-quartered in New York City. Cinchcast provides solutions for businesses to create, share, measure, and monetize audio content. Along with Bob Charish, Levy founded BlogTalkRadio (www.BlogTalkRadio.com) in August 2006. The concept for BlogTalkRadio was developed by Levy as he mourned his father's passing. Levy maintained a blog, www.theinspirationalvisit.blogspot.com, to update his family and friends on his father's health and later as a memorial to his life. Levy thought that by combining blogging and telecommunications, a true immediate two-way interactive online platform could be established. This led to the birth of BlogTalkRadio, which has become the largest online talk radio network, with more than 2 million shows broadcast since its inception.

Levy is also a principal shareholder of XChange Telecommunications, which supports the network, and is also based in New York City.

He served as president and chief operating officer of Destia Communications (NASDAQ symbol DEST) from July 1996 to December 1999. The company sold an array of communication services, including voice, data, and ISP services with sales operation in 11 countries including the U.S., U.K., and most of Western Europe. From December 1999 to March 2000, Levy was the chief operating officer at Viatel Inc. (NASDAQ symbol VYTL), a facility-based global telecommunications company. In June 1999, Viatel Inc. acquired Destia Communications in an all-stock transaction valued at $1.2 billion.

Levy graduated from Boston University with a Bachelor of Science in accounting.

I was spending a lot of time in Europe in 1998 and was at Heathrow Airport on a Friday morning on my way home to New York. I was in the Virgin Atlantic lounge when I saw Allan Shaw, a former colleague of mine who was at the time the CFO of Viatel. I had hired Allan when I was Viatel's CFO and executive vice president. Because we were number crunchers, Allan and I had always hit it off. And anytime you run into an old friend from across the pond, it's always a nice treat.

"Allan," I greeted him. "Great to see you."

"Same here, Alan," he exclaimed. "We must be on the same flight to New York."

"Viatel has been growing like gangbusters since I left," I said.

"I've been following your career," he said. "Destia has done quite well with you as its president and COO."

"Business has been good," I smiled. "And congratulations to you. How about you guys? You raised $800 million to build your European fiber network. I hear you're digging up streets all over Europe. It looks like Viatel is on its way to becoming Europe's premier provider of integrated telecommunications services."

"True," he smiled.

I knew that wasn't exactly true because I had worked there. Viatel was building a pan-European fiber optic network, which was a good thing, but it didn't have many customers. I knew that because our focus was not building networks but selling services. However, with so much competition in the marketplace, it was becoming difficult to grow our company at the same scale. We had our IPO the month before, and we had a very compelling story. Our workforce had expanded from 30 to 1,300 since I came aboard in '96, and our revenues had skyrocketed from $30 million to $350 million. We had been focusing on getting customers because we knew other companies were building networks . . . and networks need customers and traffic. Our exit strategy was to find a company with the infrastructure and cash to acquire us. I knew Viatel quite well, and I felt that it was a perfect candidate to buy Destia.

During our conversation in the airport lounge, Allan said, "I'm flying first class, and am looking forward to a relaxing trip. I could use a rest after the week I've had."

"Enjoy the flight. I'll see you in the City," I said and walked away.

I quickly went to the Virgin ticket counter and bought an upgrade so I could also be seated in first class. It cost me an extra two grand, but it was worth it if I could sit next to Allan. It would give me nearly eight hours to talk to him about why it would be a win-win for our companies to merge. Speaking of a captive audience, I thought to myself . . .

Allan boarded the plane before I did. I noticed there was an empty seat next to him. "Mind if I sit next to you?" I asked him.

"Please do," he said. "It's a long flight, and we can catch up."

Until the plane was actually in the air, our conversation was mainly small talk. Then I took out some files in my briefcase and started to review some of my papers.

"Look at this," I said to Allan. "Here are some numbers that show how our revenues have been climbing."

He looked at the file and said, "Impressive. I've been hearing through the grapevine that Destia has been building its customer base. This verifies that what I heard is correct. As you know, we've been focused on building a fiber network."

"Yes, and doing a heck of a job," I replied.

"But we don't have a sales organization in place. You guys are making great inroads throughout Europe."

"True," I said. "We built a strong sales team throughout Western Europe. We're everywhere—London, Paris, Milan." We just happened to build our sales organizations in the same major cities in Western Europe as Viatel had.

I had documents of projections in my briefcase that I showed him. I shared with him a rundown on margin analyses, and I could see he was eating it up. The fact that he's a CFO made him the perfect person for me to have as my captive audience. I knew exactly what would excite him—after all, we were both CPAs. Besides, I hired the guy. I knew what key metrics were important to him. I knew his company's strengths and weaknesses. After all, it was my former company.

We talked for the rest of the flight about the synergies that could exist if we combined forces. By the time we landed at JFK, both of us were convinced that if Destia and Viatel merged, we'd be the dominant company in the marketplace.

"I'll talk to our CEO on Monday," Allan said as we walked to the customs gate. "I think he will want to meet with you."

"It could be interesting," I answered. "And again, Allan, I enjoyed catching up with you today."

"Same here," he said. "It sure did make the time go by fast."

When I was in a taxi on my way from the airport, I called my partner and said, "I think I sold the company."

"You did? When and who's buying it?

Sure enough, the CEO called me on Monday afternoon. "Alan, I just had a long discussion with Allan Shaw this morning and he told me about the lengthy conversation he had with you flying back from London. It may make sense for us to meet to talk about what we could do with a larger company."

"I think it's a great idea," I answered.

Including debt and equity, we sold Destia in August 1999 for $1 billion. Ultimately, the value of the company went from $20 million to $1 billion. The deal closed in December 1999.

⋆ Barry's and Bob's Comments ⋆

Kudos to Alan Levy, who took the initiative to spend an extra $2,000 for a first-class ticket so he could sit next to Allan Shaw on an eight-hour flight from London to New York. As a former CFO, Levy knew that if he could sell Viatel's CFO on the value that his company represented in a merger, Shaw, in turn, would present what he heard to his CEO. Of course, having a captive audience for eight hours would have otherwise been impossible. Levy seized the moment and invested $2,000 in an upgraded ticket. Note that we say, "invested." To be sure, it was an excellent investment.

Rarely does a salesperson have the opportunity to spend so much time with a prospect to pitch his wares, so even if you were willing to pay for such an opportunity, it's improbable that you could. But you can invite a client to a fine restaurant or a round of golf to get his or her undivided attention. When such occasions are available, seize the moment!

Another lesson in this story is that sometimes you can create an interest in your product or service by selling a person who has the "ear" of the ultimate decision maker. As a CFO himself, Levy knew that if he presented a compelling story to Viatel's CFO, Shaw would have a fiduciary responsibility to report it to a senior officer. Levy also knew that due to the nature of the financial data involved, it was probable that the CEO would have to rely on his CFO's opinion and recommendations. It is worth noting that if you pitch the wrong person to get your foot in the door, it could backfire. The wrong person could do a poor job in presenting your wares and hurt your chances of making the sale!

The Method Is in the Math

Gary T. Fazio

CEO, Simmons Bedding Company

★ ★ ★

Gary Fazio joined Simmons Bedding Company, head-quartered in Atlanta, in July 2010 as its chief executive officer. In this capacity, he oversees the company's sales, marketing, and manufacturing functions in the United States, Puerto Rico, and Canada, where Simmons operates 20 plants. From 2001 to 2010 when he joined Simmons, Fazio was CEO of a retailer with more than 700 stores. He had also served as its chairman for six months in 2010. He has held several top-level sales and marketing positions in the bedding industry since 1972.

Fazio began his career as a bedding and sleep sofa buyer for Federated Department Stores. He graduated from The Ohio

SUCCESS SECRETS OF SALES SUPERSTARS

State University in 1972 with a B.A. in speech communications. Fazio received the 2011 Anti-Defamation League American Heritage Award and established The Annette and Gary T. Fazio Scholarship Foundation at The Ohio State University and the North Carolina State University.

★ ★ ★

Back in the 1990s, I was senior vice president of sales with a mattress manufacturer that was number one in U.S. market share. The company had brought in a new CEO, and a few months later, I met with him to present a business plan that I thought would determine the company's future as the industry's market leader.

When we met, a lot of things were happening in the industry, and I believed that our company had some unique opportunities, but to capitalize on them, we'd have to aggressively move in a new direction. If not, those opportunities would no longer be available. This meant that I had to convince the new CEO that we were at a crossroads where major change was inevitable and if we sat tight and did little to make a paradigm shift, there could be severe consequences.

I started by telling him, "I realize that you have been here a relatively short time, and there is a lot on your plate that you have to digest. If I had my druthers, I would have preferred to wait until you had more time under your belt as CEO before I presented what I have to say to you. But time doesn't permit it, sir. As we speak, several major things are happening with two of our biggest customers as well as two large retailers whose mattress business we have been actively pursuing. I remind you, sir, that these two customers exclusively sell our mattresses. I feel it is imperative that we must make some big decisions on how to deal with each of these situations because these are decisions that cannot be delayed. If we don't do what I believe requires immediate action, it is probable that we will deeply regret it later on."

9 / Fazio: The Method Is in the Math

I could see from his expression that, at the very least, my statement got his attention. He sat erectly in his chair, and leaning forward said, "Go ahead, Gary, I'm listening."

"We cannot afford to lose the business of our major customers," I said.

He listened intently and said, "I am aware of their importance to this company, and yes, I agree."

"Now although the circumstances differ with each of these companies," I explained, "we must make specific commitments to each of them. We must do it swiftly or we will risk losing significant revenues and, in turn, losing our number-one position in market share in the U.S. bedding industry."

"How do you know that?" he asked.

I had thoroughly done my homework and was very familiar with two of these big customers because I had personally worked with them over the years, and the CEO knew this. I was aware that he had an excellent furniture industry background, but he had only been running a mattress company for a short while. I also knew that I was presenting a lot of major issues all at once, and my years of sales experience had taught me that you shouldn't overwhelm anyone with too many facts. And if you do, it will make decision making more difficult. But because there was so much going on in our industry at the time, I had no choice. Fortunately, our CEO was a respected and experienced furniture executive, so I could rely on his business acumen to take it all in and make an intelligent decision. Knowing this, I decided to make a brief presentation on each of the companies, explaining how each had a different set of circumstances.

"Company A," I pointed out, "is in an expansion mode. It is opening stores across the country, and if we cater to its needs, the volume of business it does with us will substantially increase. If we continue to do business as usual, our relationship could be jeopardized."

"What are you proposing we must do?" he asked.

"There are several things," I said, "some of which will require us to invest money in its expansion; other things we can do will require our time and expertise. For instance, we will have to invest money in grand openings of new stores. This will require advertising and promotion dollars, floor displays, training salespeople, and so on. We will advise the company on store locations, share information on demographics, and help it set up its bedding departments.

"Company B is interested in having a high-quality mattress that will be sold exclusively in its stores," I continued. "We are currently constructing a mattress for them that we had made in Europe, and it believes its quality is responsible for its bedding success. It has never been made in the United States, and its patent has expired. We can now make the mattress domestically under a different brand name. If we do this for this customer, they will be elated, and here, too, the amount of business we do with it will increase."

I explained what Company C and Company D required, and again, these would require significant commitments from our company.

"As you can see, they all want to grow their companies," I went on. "And when they expand, if we are their main source, we will realize substantial growth. Look at the upside. We will increase our sales volume with two of our biggest accounts, and we will open two large accounts. Now look at the downside. If we do nothing, we could expect to lose sales that will go to our competition. It is also likely that if we lose some or all of their business, our market share will drop. We will no longer have our number-one position in the bedding industry, and as you know, that would have severe consequences."

"Do you want to elaborate on those consequences?" he asked.

"After you tumble to number two in an industry that you dominated," I explained, "people begin to believe that you are vulnerable, and they will start walking away from you in more ways than you can even put on paper. Who knows what the innuendo will be when people see that we fell from being number one! That's something we don't want to find out."

This was a threat to all of us, not just my CEO but to me, too. It was something that I took very personally.

"By doing all that they are asking," he questioned, "how can we be sure we will get more business from each of them?"

"In the past, we have never had a contractual arrangement with our customers," I answered. "It's always been an oral agreement in this industry. These customers aren't used to signing binding agreements. It's been, 'If we do this, we will expect you to do this.' With the big commitments we will make to these companies, we will ask them to give us something in return. We will put in writing what we will do, and in turn, they will sign agreements with us that commit them to sell our mattresses."

"But if this has never been done before in the bedding industry," he said, "do you think they will sign contracts with us?"

"It will be a first in the bedding industry, but I believe that they will."

"Why so?" he asked.

"I think they will realize that they are better off with a contract," I said. "It will be protection for both sides. It's a win-win. They will realize that the only way they can get such a terrific offering from us as well as a long-term commitment from our organization is for them to pony up, and part of that is agreeing to it in writing."

"Are you so sure they'll go along with it?"

"I have worked with the two retailers for a long time, and I know them very well," I said. "Yes, sir, I am confident they will."

With that, I pulled out a single sheet of paper that I had prepared before the meeting. "Here it is on paper," I said, showing him the numbers that we did with each of the four companies. "Now here in this left column is what I project our sales volumes will be with each company if we go forward. And in this right column is what I project we will do if we don't. As you can see, there are substantial differences in how we will gain or lose business."

He looked at the paper and said, "These are huge differences."

"We're swinging for the fences," I said, "and if we miss, we not only don't get a home run, we can lose a lot of money."

The CEO studied the numbers.

Had I talked about each customer individually, his reaction might have been, "We better not do that. We've never done anything like that before." And on another one, it could have been, "We should pass on this one. We've never made those kinds of mattresses." And on the next one, "We have never worked economically with a retailer like this, and we better not now." But by putting the numbers on one piece of paper and spelling out what the consequences were if we kept the status quo, it was obvious that we couldn't stand still; remaining stationary was tantamount to going backward. Although the CEO was new in the mattress industry, he recognized that the risk of falling into second place in market share was a disturbing option. He also understood that the bedding business was a low-barrier-to-enter industry and a competitor could quickly come along and take our position.

By putting it on one piece of paper, it became a stark reality that if we didn't do what I suggested, the consequences were greater than the risk of doing them and not making money. It was obvious that we couldn't do it piecemeal because all of the opportunities were happening at the same time. There was a go-or-no-go scenario. It wasn't as if we could sit and wait and do them at our leisure. All of these customers had circumstances in which they were making decisions at the same time. Plus there were competitors trying to get their business, seeking to make deals with them with the standard methodologies. What I proposed would change the paradigm of doing business in the bedding industry.

I'm a big metric person. I believe the method is in the math, but not only the math. If you look at the mathematics, it usually proves out the facts. In this case, on a single sheet of paper, I showed the math—on the left side was *what if*. On the right side was *what if not*. It spelled out what our market share would be if we got those deals and what the competitors' market share would be if we didn't get those deals.

The CEO looked at the sheet of paper. He nodded and said decisively, "Go for it."

Aware that the clock was ticking, it was urgent that we act quickly. We made an all-or-nothing decision and aggressively moved forward. We signed our two big customers as well as one of the two large retailers, so we batted .750. Announcements were made in the trade journals, and when the word got out, other major retailers came to us wanting to sign written agreements with the same kinds of commitments. As a consequence, we propelled our growth and our profits soared.

★ Barry's and Bob's Comments ★

It was a bold move for Gary Fazio to make this presentation to his new boss. Gary was putting his entire career on the line. However, he did what he had to do—and he did it with conviction. He was well prepared when he walked into his meeting with the CEO. He had done his homework and clearly presented the facts. Note that he didn't overwhelm the CEO with tear sheets, charts, and statistics. By organizing his presentation on a single sheet of paper that listed the potential gains in the left column and the potential losses in the right column, he concisely presented his case in an uncomplicated way. He explained the gravity of the situation, and this enabled the CEO to make a decision to move forward. Note, too, that Gary created a sense of urgency by illustrating to his boss that time was of the essence. The company was in jeopardy of losing substantial revenues if it didn't take immediate action. He emphasized that a lot was at stake and indecisiveness could result in a severe setback for the company.

Persistence Pays Off

Craig R. Smith

Chairman, Swiss America Trading Corporation

★ ★ ★

*C*raig Smith founded Swiss America Trading Corporation, *a Phoenix-based investment firm that specializes in U.S. gold and silver coins, in 1982. With annual revenues in excess of $300 million in 2010, Swiss America is one of the largest and most respected firms in the industry. Considered an expert in many forms of tangible assets including oil, precious metals, and U.S. numismatic (collectible) coins, Smith is a media favorite, often making guest appearances on national radio and TV to share his insights on world events and financial trends. He is a frequent guest on Fox's* Your World with Neil Cavuto *and on* Harvest TV's Money Moment. *He writes a weekly editorial for*

Worldnetdaily.com and a monthly one for Real Money Perspectives *newsletter.*

★ ★ ★

After learning the business while working at another company, I started Swiss America in 1982. I began with $50 and worked out of a bedroom in my home. An average trade was $50,000 to $100,000, and after a client paid us, we had a week to ten days to make the delivery. This gave me enough time to buy the product and make the delivery. My business took off and within two years, I had hired several salespeople and a small office staff.

One day, T.J. Blake (a fictitious name), a wealthy industrialist from the West Coast, called, and we did a $135,000 trade. Along with a $100,000 check, he sent some Krugerrands he wanted me to sell and asked me to buy some early American gold coins for him. The coins were delivered a few days later.

A couple of weeks went by and I got a phone call from him. "Smith? This is T.J. Blake."

"Good morning, Mr. Blake. How are you today?"

"Where's my $35,000?"

I was swamped with orders because back then we didn't have the systems in place that we do today. I didn't recall the status of his account, so I asked, "What do you mean, sir?"

"I sent you $135,000 and you only sent me $100,000 worth of coins. What about the American gold coins due me for my Krugerrands?"

"Mr. Blake, I don't know what happened. Let me do some checking around here, and I'll call you back. I assure you, if there is a mistake, I will correct it immediately."

"You've got my number, and I'll be here waiting for your call," he said abruptly.

"Sandy, what's going on?" I asked my secretary. "We were supposed to send $35,000 to T.J. Blake, and it seems he never received it. Can you pull his file and give me the status on it?"

"Boss, we got a little ahead of ourselves," she said softly.

"What's that mean?" I asked.

"You're backed up in your deliveries," she answered. "We've done so much business that we're having a cash flow problem. Mr. Blake is correct: We owe him $35,000, but we don't have the cash in our account right now to write him a check to cover it. We'll be okay, sir. When the money comes in that's due us, we'll be able to pay him."

Sandy handed me some financial papers, and I felt a chill go up and down my spine. I knew we were making money, but we didn't have the funds for the money due Blake. I had a serious problem, and I could do one of two things. I could find $35,000 to return to Blake or find a product to sell him that would make a $35,000 profit to cover what I owed him. I figured the best solution was to sell him some additional coins.

"Mr. Blake, this is Craig Smith," I said. "You were right. There's a $35,000 difference that's due you. I will put in the paperwork and get it out to you in the next day or two. I apologize for causing you a problem."

He said that was fine, and this allowed me to buy some time to come up with a solution. After making some calls to my contacts in the industry, I talked to a prominent rare coin dealer in Sherman Oaks, California, who had two truly rare coins—an 1862 double eagle and an 1865 double eagle. These were super rare coins that couldn't be found elsewhere.

I called Mr. Blake and said, "I'm putting your check together. But meantime, I came across an 1862 and an 1865 double eagle, and I can let you have them for $135,000. This will complete our transaction."

"Man, that's terrific," Blake said. "I love those coins."

I sensed he might not trust me due to the mix-up so I said, "I'll just jump on a plane and deliver them to you. I've heard a lot of good things about you, and this will give us an opportunity to meet in person."

"Sounds good," he said. "I'm looking forward to seeing you and those double eagles."

Two hours later, Blake called me. "This is Blake," he said in a harsh voice. "I don't want those coins. I could buy them for $120,000 in Beverly Hills. I don't want any nonsense from you. Just send me my money."

Blake might have called another coin dealer in the area who gave him a lower price, but I didn't think that was possible. The two coins were so rare that they weren't available elsewhere. I purposely chose those two coins because I knew it would be practically impossible to shop around to compare prices. The dealer Blake spoke to was obviously thinking he'd buy the same coins I had already reserved from the Sherman Oaks dealer.

"Mr. Blake, you and I have an appointment tomorrow morning, and I've already purchased my airline ticket. I know you're a man of your word. I'll see you at 9:00 A.M. tomorrow." With that, I hung up the phone and took the receiver off the hook.

I took an early morning flight out of Phoenix to L.A., rushed over to Sherman Oaks, picked up the double eagles, and drove down to Blake's house. In my briefcase was a check for $35,000 and the two coins. Blake's daughter, Missy, answered the door. She told me that she was a financial planner and represented her father. "Craig, my dad doesn't want to meet with you. He just wants his $35,000, so give it to me. There is nothing to talk about."

"I have a meeting with your father. Would you please have him come to the door?" I said.

I stood having a heated exchange with Missy Blake for about 20 minutes, and finally she let me in. Blake and I sat down at the kitchen table. I was there to make a sale that I desperately needed. We were so cash-strapped, the future of my company depended on this deal. We talked for about an hour, and Blake said, "Smith, I don't want to see those coins. I just want my money."

"Mr. Blake, I'm not even going to show you the coins," I told him. "The way I've been treated in this house . . ."

At this point Mrs. Blake walked into the room and said to me, "I want you out of my house," and she showed me to the front door and slammed it as I walked out. I rang the doorbell, and nobody answered. I knocked hard on the door, but still, no reply. I was persistent because

I had to get back into the house. I started to think, "What am I doing? They're going to call the police if I don't let up." But I kept knocking on the door, knowing I had to get inside so I could convince Blake to accept those coins.

Missy came to the door, and I said to her, "This is ridiculous. If nothing else, I have to get inside the house to give your father his check because I want his signature that he received it." Reluctantly, she allowed me in.

Blake was visibly upset. "I need a cigarette," he said. "Come outside with me to the garden so I can smoke."

When he said this, I observed something I hadn't noticed before. Blake was a successful and wealthy businessman who ran his company with an iron hand. At the office, he barked orders and was the master of his universe. But at home, his wife and daughter henpecked him.

"Why are we going outside?" I asked.

"My wife doesn't allow me to smoke in the house."

"Are you kidding me? A man of your stature and you have to go outside to have a cigarette?"

His face reddened and he firmly said, "I could have a cigarette wherever I damn please in this house," and with that, he lit up a cigarette at the kitchen table.

Now I realized I had to play to his manliness. "You know what I'm going to do, Mr. Blake, I'm going to break one of my rules, and I'm going to show you these coins." I put them on the table and watched his eyes light up. I knew then that I was close. Now I had to get him to take out his checkbook and write a check for $100,000.

"I'd love to be a man with your means, Mr. Blake," I said, "because if I could afford these coins, I'd buy them myself. These coins are so rare that someday you might even want to donate them to the Smithsonian, which, as you know, has one of the most outstanding coin collections in the world." I truly believed that if the markets continued to perform as they had in the past, Mr. Blake would in time make a very nice profit.

Just then, his wife walked into the room. I thought to myself, "Oh no, what bad timing." But before she could say a word, he sent her to her bedroom. Then his daughter came in. "Missy, I'll take care of this. Don't worry about it. You just head back home. I got this under control."

Around 3:30 in the afternoon, he pulled out his checkbook. "I like the coins," he said.

It had been a long day. I hadn't taken a bathroom break, eaten lunch, or even had a glass of water. At this point, I stopped talking about coins, and we talked about everything from flyfishing to how he loved to work with his employees in the shop. Even when he started talking about the coins, I continued to talk about everything but business. By the end of the day, we were just two guys having a good old time talking together.

`Blake handed the check to me and said, "Thank you, Craig. I can't tell you how much I enjoyed talking to you."

After I left the house, I drove straight to the bank to get a cashier's check so I could pay for the coins. I also wanted to make sure Blake didn't change his mind and stop payment on the check. Just as I pulled up to the bank, the branch manager was locking up for the day. "Sorry," I was told, "you'll have to come back tomorrow morning. We're closed."

I called a friend who was attending a coin show in L.A., and he said I could sleep in the twin bed in his hotel room that night. Otherwise, I would have had to sleep in my rental car because I didn't have enough cash to pay for a room and my credit cards were maxed out.

The next morning, I was the first to walk into the bank when the door opened. "I have a check for $100,000 from Mr. Blake, one of your big customers," I told the teller. "I need you to turn it into a cashier's check."

"I'm sorry, but I have to call over the manager for a check that size," I was told.

The manager came over and said, "I'm sorry, but with a check in this amount, I have to call Mr. Blake for his approval."

Now I'm thinking, "Oh, great. Blake has the coins, and I'm holding a piece of paper that the manager can tell me is no good."

"Is there a phone I can use?" I said.

At a desk across the room, I quickly dialed Blake before the manager could call him. "Mr. Blake, this is Craig."

"How you doing, Craig? Say, I'm really enjoying my coins."

"That's great," I said, and we chatted a while. Then I said, "I spent the night in L.A., and I'm now at your bank. You won't believe what's going on. If I didn't know any better, and no offense, sir, but these people treat your account like you're some small fish. I thought you were one of the bank's biggest customers."

"What are you talking about?"

"Well, they're giving me a hard time. The manager..."

"You put that son-of-a-bitch on the phone," he interrupted.

I waved my arms and caught the eye of the manager on the other side of the room. He came over, and I handed him the phone.

I heard him saying, "Yes, Mr. Blake . . . I apologize, Mr. Blake . . . Yes, sir, I'll take care of it. Thank you, sir."

With that, he signed his initials on a corner of the check and said to the teller, "Give him a cashier's check."

I was so high, I didn't need a plane to fly back to Phoenix. Had I not got the sale, I was prepared to tell Blake about the cash flow problem we were having and explain, "Sir, if you are willing to work with me, I will take all of the profits on my next trades and send you a check every week like clockwork, and I will also pay you interest on the money." A couple of years later, I actually had to do that with another client when we were in another cash-starved situation.

About ten years later, Blake sold the two coins for $265,000.

★ Barry's and Bob's Comments ★

We think every professional salesperson should be able to relate to Craig Smith's story because at one time or another, we've all been in the same boat, desperately needing to make a sale as if our life depended on it. And who hasn't had a marathon sale that dragged on for hours? Believe us when we tell you that it's no fun to confront a belligerent customer the likes of Smith's Mr. Blake. It is part of the sales game. If you can't take the heat—get out of the kitchen! If closing every big sale were easy, everyone would be in sales. However, as we all know, most people don't have the intestinal fortitude to endure what Smith went through to make this sale. It's sales like this that separate the truly professional salesperson from the novice. Sometimes you have to be tenacious and hang in there until you get the job done. And when you do, it's good for your customer and you!

The Power of Transparency

Phillip R. Styrlund

CEO, The Summit Group

★ ★ ★

*P*hillip *Styrlund heads* The Summit Group, *a premier consulting and sales training firm based in Minneapolis. The Summit Group's clients include Fortune 500 companies such as American Express, AT&T, Cisco, GlaxoSmithKline, Hewlett Packard, Motorola, Ritz-Carlton, 3M, and Xerox. The company also consults with the federal government. Phil has written for, and been cited in, leading publications such as the* Wall Street Journal, National Account Management Journal, *and* Fast Company. *He is the author of* Adversity Quotient *and* The Power of Purpose. *He serves as a coach, mentor, consultant, and advisor to top leaders across a wide range of industries.*

★ ★ ★

B
ack in 1985, I was working for U.S. West, one of the Baby Bells spun off after the AT&T breakup. The company had a handful of strategic accounts in the Twin Cities that included Control Data, Honeywell, General Mills, Northwest Airlines, Medtronic, and 3M.

Ron James, the local CEO for U.S. West in Minnesota, asked me to come to his office for a conference. "Phil, we're having some major problems with Control Data and are on the verge of losing the account," James said. "It's one of our biggest customers, and we want to retain their business."

I had a technical role at the time and didn't understand why he was telling this to me, so I just listened. Then James dropped a bombshell. "I'm putting you in charge of the account, Phil. You will be our strategic account manager handling Control Data."

"I'll do what?" I asked in surprise. "Ron, that's a senior sales position, and I've never been in sales before."

"It doesn't matter," he said. "I know you'll do just fine."

James explained that my job would be to salvage our business with Control Data, a relationship that had deteriorated over the years. He stressed that in terms of revenue Control Data was probably one of our top three accounts, so a lot was riding on keeping the company as a customer. He said that he had full confidence that I could save the account. While James might have had confidence in me, I certainly did not! How could I? I had never sold anything in my life. I was in my late 20s and had no clue what I should do.

At the time, we had a Control Data office located in the U.S. West offices, so the first thing I did was to move my office to its premises. Not only did I put my office inside Control Data, I also made sure it was on the same floor, just a few doors down from the customer, its Telecommunications Group and IT organization. I spent my first two days there just listening to all of the problems, issues, and challenges we had with this account. It seemed overwhelming, and I kept thinking, "What did I get myself into?"

On the third day, I went to a local office supply store and bought the biggest whiteboard in stock. It was five feet by seven feet. I put it up on my office wall and invited the two key players on the customer's side to come in. These gentlemen were Bill Miller, director of IT and Telecommunications, and Harry Hurley, manager of Telecommunications. They were the key decision makers. They were the customer. Period.

I asked them to tell me everything they considered to be problems. I listened intently, and then I said, "I'm brand-new. I've never been in sales. Guys, tell me what to do. How should we go about mending this relationship? What needs to happen?"

At first, they didn't know what to make of me. "The more you can share with me," I stressed, "the more I can help you. I can't fix things I don't know about."

They talked, and I listened. After they were finished, I said, "I've got this big whiteboard here, so let's make it simple. Take this pen, draw out what needs to happen, and list the things that we need to get done. As each gets taken care of, we'll wipe it off, and when that whiteboard is clean, our relationship will be clean."

They consented, and for the next few hours we filled the whiteboard with everything we needed to do to mend the relationship and help them serve their internal customers. When we were finished, we agreed that the three of us would meet at least once a week, and during these meetings, we would sit in front of that whiteboard and wipe off items that had been resolved, if we all agreed they were complete.

We wrote action items and issues on the whiteboard, and it became my relational to-do list. Each time we'd meet in my office, we'd check off a couple of things that were no longer problems. The entire tenor of the previous relationship had changed. It was no longer an adversarial relationship that pitted us against them. Now it was us vs. the challenges. We worked together in a true partnership. Finally at the end of two months, we checked off the final item on the whiteboard. The whiteboard was clean, and the relationship had been cleaned up. The three of us celebrated and went out to have a beer. I've been good friends with Bill and Harry ever since.

I was promoted to head of strategic accounts throughout the Midwest. In this capacity, I was in charge of strategic account managers who worked with U.S. West's major customers—3M, Honeywell, General Mills, all the big ones. Based on what I learned from my Control Data experience, I decided to use that same approach with other accounts. Knowing that relationships were so critical to our company, whenever I hired the key people for one of our account teams, including the strategic account manager, I invited the customer to participate in the interviewing process. This way, instead of saying, "This is your new strategic account manager who will handle your account," I'd say, "Let's do this together so we can figure out who is the right person for the job. After all, you should be involved in choosing the right person because you'll be working with him more than I."

The customers were always agreeable, so I'd bring in the two or three final candidates. Then we'd interview them together, and afterward, we'd meet to decide who would be the best strategic account manager. When I did this, two things happened: First, by getting them involved, I couldn't be wrong. Second, because they were involved in the process, they wanted to make that person successful. I've applied this approach ever since. As a consultant, my advice to my clients is: "Outsource your customer. Let the customer solve problems for you." It's so much easier. I truly believe that a salesperson's job is to create a vehicle that lets the customer solve his own problems. That's really the bottom line. Let them self-solve.

Admittedly, it is difficult for most salespeople to relate to my self-solve philosophy. That's because they have been taught, "It's all about you." You have been told, "You're the man." In truth, it is not about you, and the more you can get out of the way of yourself, the more things in life snap together and come toward you. This is one of the most difficult things in life. Our insecurities drive our need to put ourselves in the middle when the greater truth is, it is not about us. The more you get out of your own way, the more the way becomes clear. It is simply operationalizing the platinum rule . . . do unto others as they want to have done to themselves. Further, let them tell you what they want. In essence, let them help you help them. Lead from the center of their needs, not the middle of your needs. Worry less about dazzling people with your competence and more about being interested in their concerns. Simply be interested, not interesting.

⋆ Barry's and Bob's Comments ⋆

As many of our stories reveal, some of the most effective selling doesn't seem like selling at all. That is, not in the traditional sense, in which you try to convince a customer to buy your product or service and the more resistance you get, the harder you sell. In this story, Styrlund wisely avoided the stereotypical "us vs. them" relationship, one that puts the salesperson and the customer at opposite sides of the spectrum. Instead, he advocates a teamwork philosophy that encourages both parties to work together to solve a mutual problem. Styrlund takes it a step further by recommending that a salesperson should let the customer solve the problem. We agree with him when he says that your job as a salesperson is to create the vehicle that lets the customer self-solve. We believe that when a customer becomes involved in finding a solution to his problem, he takes ownership, which is the foundation to a solid salesperson-customer relationship.

Letting the Customer Know He's Important to You

Richard Santulli

Chairman of the Board, Milestone Aviation Group

★ ★ ★

In 2009 Richard Santulli co-founded Milestone Aviation Group and was named chairman of the board. Milestone is a global aviation leasing company based in the United States and Ireland. It provides financing to the helicopter and private jet markets around the world.

Santulli is the former CEO of NetJets, a Columbus, Ohio-based company he purchased in 1984. Santulli is recognized as the man who shaped the face of private aviation when he devised the first-ever fractional aircraft ownership plan. In August 2009, when he left NetJets, it was a wholly owned subsidiary of Berkshire Hathaway and the largest private aviation company in the world.

It had a fleet of more than 800 aircraft, annual revenue in excess of $4 billion, and more than 7,000 employees around the world.

Prior to starting NetJets, Santulli owned RTS Helicopters, which he built into the world's largest helicopter lessor. At its peak, RTS had nearly 200 machines under lease. It specialized in serving offshore oil and gas leases, mainly in the Gulf of Mexico. From 1969 to 1980, he was an investment banker at Goldman Sachs & Co., where he started and served as president of the firm's leasing business unit for proprietary equipment, including software and technology.

Santulli earned B.S. and M.S. degrees in applied mathematics at Brooklyn Polytechnic Institute and graduated in 1966.

He has served as the chairman of the Intrepid Fallen Heroes Fund since 2003. Under his leadership, the fund has provided more than $100 million in support of veterans and military families and built the Center for the Intrepid at the Brooke Army Medical Centre in San Antonio, Texas, as well as the National Intrepid Center of Excellence, which opened in June 2010 in Washington, DC. Santulli also serves on the board of directors at the Mercy Home for Children, the Andre Agassi Charitable Foundation, The Jockey Club, and the Breeders' Cup.

★ ★ ★

Whenever someone had a problem with a customer, our people knew I was on-call 24/7. Back in 1998, I received such a call from Steve Eiseman, one of NetJets' top salespeople. Steve didn't hesitate to call me on this particular Saturday morning because he knew I'd be there for him.

"I've got a problem with a customer," Steve told me, "and I need your help."

"Go ahead, I'm listening."

"Ray Catena is one of my prospects," he said. "You know him, Rich. He owns and operates large automobile dealerships all over New Jersey; there's one near where you live. His franchises sell Lexus, Mercedes, Aston Martin, Jaguar, Porsche, and Infiniti all over the state."

"Yes, I know the company," I replied. "Catena is always at the top of any list that ranks dealerships on customer satisfaction. It's known for its superior service to its customers. I'm sure he expects the same service from others, too."

"He does," Steve interjected, "and this is why he's planning to go with FlexJets."

"Catena is really close to where I live," I said. "Come on, Steve. I don't want to lose this account. What can I do to save it?"

"I'd love it if you'd talk to him, Rich. Maybe something you say can save this account."

"Have any idea why he's unhappy with us?" I asked.

"He thinks we're getting too big," Steve answered. "He thinks we won't care about him like a smaller company would."

"That's not true," I said.

"Sure, I know that, Rich. But like I said, that's what he thinks."

"Tell Ray to call me on my cell number. Call him back now, and let him know I am expecting to hear from him."

"Will do," Steve said.

The date was March 7, 1998. A few minutes later, the phone rings, and it's him. "Hey, Rich, this is Ray Catena. I'm sorry to bother you on a Saturday morning, but Steve Eiseman said I should and you'd be waiting for my call. Otherwise I would have let it wait until Monday morning."

I walked outside with my phone. "I'm glad you did," I said. "Steve said you had a problem, Ray, and I'd like to know about it. Maybe I could help."

"Look, I know you guys are safe, your prices are fair, and all that, but look, Rich, I'm in the service business too. I decided to go with Flex, which is much smaller than NetJets. That's all."

"Go on," I said.

"I like the fact that Flex is small," he continued, "and this is why I think I'd be better off with them. You're so big, Rich, and I'll be just a little fish in a big pond."

"I'll tell you what, Ray," I said. "I'll give you a million dollars if you can tell me what I'm going to do in one hour from now. I'm serious, $1 million."

"What are you talking about?" he asked.

"You heard me, and I mean it. If you can tell me what I will be doing in one hour from now, I will give you a certified check for $1 million."

"Okay," he said. "The weather is warm today. You'll be playing golf."

"Wrong answer. Want to guess again?"

"You'll be having your lunch?"

"Wrong."

"Brunch?

"Wrong again."

"You're playing tennis?"

"That's not it either."

"You're going fishing."

"Again, wrong answer."

"Going boating?"

"No."

"For crying out loud, Rich, I give up. What will you be doing one hour from now?"

"I'm getting married."

"You're getting married?" he asked in surprise.

"That's right. I'm getting married in my house. I'm outside on the lawn. Say, Ray, would you like to come to the wedding? In one hour the priest will be here. You're close enough that you can make it."

"You're serious, aren't you?"

"Absolutely," I replied. "And you said we don't care about our customers."

"Rich, would you please tell Steve to send me the contract? And congratulations on your marriage. I wish I could come today, but I can't make it. But thanks for the invitation."

★ Barry's and Bob's Comments ★

By taking the time to talk to a customer on his wedding day, Santulli made it clear that taking care of customers was a top priority. It wasn't that Ray Catena objected to doing business with big companies—he owned one himself. What he wanted was assurance that NetJets had not become so big that he would no longer receive personal attention by the company.

We've all been treated like a number by big companies that have lost the personal touch. We get that impersonal treatment when we call to make airline reservations and are put on hold by computers. It takes much too long to talk to a "live" person, and to most of us, it's incredibly frustrating. Utility companies, telephone companies, catalog companies, and all kinds of other service companies have low-paid employees working somewhere in third-world countries who speak broken English and are poorly trained to handle complaints. People are fed up with big companies that seem unwilling to spend the money and take the time to hear their problems, let alone solve their problems. Why should a customer care about a company he feels doesn't care about him? Richard Santulli showed that he cared about his customer, and that's why he won the customer's loyalty.

This story is a particularly good lesson for the owner of a startup company—or for that matter, any entrepreneur. People like to deal with the owner of a company. Think about how you feel when you go into a small retail store and the owner personally waits on you, knows your name, and thanks you for your business. It could be a small men's haberdashery, a ladies' boutique, or a small independent bookstore. Or it could be the owner of a restaurant who greets you by name when you walk in or comes to your table and asks you if everything is okay. And if something went wrong, he offers a round of drinks or desserts on the house. The owner or manager makes a customer feel important. It's a personal touch that customers cherish. When the owner thanks a customer for her business, it's as if the entire company is thanking her. Sadly, small-business owners often don't understand this concept and consequently fail to capitalize on what could be their biggest advantage over their big competitors.

Truly great companies with dominant market share work overtime to make sure they always think small. The bigger they get, the harder they work to treat everyone like they did when they were small, fledgling companies, building their base of loyal customers.

God's Gift to Women

Barbara Sunden

Number-One National Sales Director Mary Kay Inc.

★ ★ ★

M ary Kay Inc., the renowned cosmetics company, has more than 2 million women in its sales force selling its products in 38 countries around the world. Barbara Sunden is the company's number-one sales leader. For five consecutive years, her annual commissions have exceeded $1 million.

In April 1972, Barbara started her Mary Kay career as a beauty consultant, as does every other member in the sales force starting out with the company. She became a sales director in October 1973 and one year later became a senior director. In June 1978, she was voted Miss Go Give, a recognition given to the individual in the *sales organization who distinguishes herself for her giving spirit. This honor is among the most coveted awards presented at the company's annual sales conference in Dallas.*

Barbara became a national sales director in 1982 and a senior national sales director in 1984. Today, she has ten national sales directors in her sales organization; this distinction has earned her the title elite executive national sales director. It is estimated that there are more than 20,000 members in her sales organization. Barbara is also a charter member of the President's Club and a member of the Inner Circle, an honor she has had for 24 consecutive years.

Barbara's sales organization has expanded to seven countries. In addition to the United States, it is represented in Canada, the United Kingdom, Mexico, Brazil, South Korea, and the Philippines. She and her husband Richard reside in Old Tappan, New Jersey.

☆ ☆ ☆

I became a Mary Kay beauty consultant in 1972 because I loved the product and I enjoyed conducting skin-care classes. I did it just for fun and quit three months later when my son was born. At the time, it was just another sales job.

My experience reminds me of a story about two railroad workers who were sitting on a bench having lunch. The president of the company walked by and said hello to one of the men, and they talked briefly. After the president left, the other worker asked, "How do you know the president of the company so well?"

"He and I both came to work for the railroad at the same time," he answered, "and we worked side by side doing manual labor."

"Yes, but he's the company president now. You're still at the same job."

"That's true," the man replied. "When I started here, I came to work to earn $1.40 an hour. He came to work to build a railroad."

This story reminds me about my first tenure with Mary Kay. When I started, I only knew about the product line, and I came to sell cosmetics. At the time, the company's values and its culture had never been explained to me. Later I found out, and I recognized that there was a vast opportunity for me if I was willing to work hard to earn it. I was determined to build a business, not just conduct skin-care classes. I still loved the products, and I swear by them to this day. But I realized I wasn't in the cosmetics business. I was in a business that provided opportunities to women.

When Mary Kay Ash, the founder of our company, was alive and active in the business, I was fortunate to get to know her personally because she worked closely with the elite group of national sales directors, who she referred to as her daughters. She groomed us to follow her lead so that when she was no longer here we'd spread the word on what the company was all about. "It's about people," she'd say. "The product is the vehicle, but the people are the mission." I've applied this philosophy throughout my career, and it is to what I attribute my success.

With this mind-set, when I recruit someone to join my sales organization, I don't just sell her on the wonderful skin-care products the company has. Instead I focus on the value I can add to her life. I emphasize the career opportunity that is available and how it can improve her life. As an example of how this works, when Mary Kay was launched in Canada in 1978, I went there a few months after the grand opening. I was in a coffee shop, and I spotted this other young lady who looked as if she was in deep thought. I went over and introduced myself.

"Hi, my name is Barbara Sunden," I said. "Do you mind if I join you?"

"Please do," she volunteered. "I'm Tricia."

"I couldn't help noticing that you looked like you have a lot on your mind," I said.

"You got that right," she said. After exchanging pleasantries she told me about how she had just broken up from a relationship and was contemplating ways that she might completely change her life. "I'm thinking about moving to England and starting all over."

She continued to talk and then asked, "Look at me, I'm telling my life's story to somebody I never met before. Yet I feel comfortable doing it." She paused briefly and asked, "This is all so strange. Tell me, Barbara, what made you come over to my table and talk to me? And tell me what brings you to Toronto."

I explained that I was a senior sales director for Mary Kay Cosmetics, and I briefly talked about the skin-care products we sold. She asked some questions, and then I talked to her about the opportunities that were available to women in our organization. "You asked me why I came over to talk to you," I said, "and I'm not really sure I know. You can call it fate, or perhaps it was woman's intuition. I just saw the concerned expression you had on your face, and I felt compelled to talk to you."

"I can't tell you how much I appreciate your interest in me," she said.

"And the timing is so right," I replied. "You are looking for a major change in your life, so you might want to consider a career with our company. Based on my first impression, I think you would do very well in this business."

Tricia didn't make a commitment that day, but we connected. We exchanged contact information, and a little later she came aboard. She quickly became a top producer, and in fact, she was named the company's number-one sales director several times. And as a result of meeting Tricia in that coffee shop, I have four national sales directors in Canada!

Now, what something inside of me was it that urged me to introduce myself to her? Had I not done so, Tricia's life would have taken an entirely different direction. But something did, and boy, did it change her life in a positive way. If this had only happened this one time or only a few times during my long Mary Kay career, I probably wouldn't give much thought to it. However, it has happened so many times that I learned to take it quite seriously, and most importantly, I act on it. It's one thing to have a gut feeling and ignore it. I believe that you have to follow up on it. Opportunities to meet people happen all the time. Sadly, in a situation like my encounter with Tricia, most people would only fantasize about approaching a person who looked interesting and follow through by engaging in a conversation. So while their gut might have sent a message to them, they ignore it. You have to believe in messages your gut sends you, and you must take the initiative to act on it.

Then there was another time when Mary Kay Inc. was opening in the Philippines in 2000. I was invited to the grand opening, and different events were held around the country, each attended by thousands of guests. At the time, we had no representation there. My reason for going was to support the company, and at one event, as a national sales director, I was asked to say a few words. When I got up to speak, I said, "I came to the Philippines to help with the business opening, but instead I fell in love with the people here." I talked for a little more but don't remember saying anything significant. Later, I was approached by a woman in the audience who had a friend who worked at our corporate offices. "I liked what you just said about how you fell in love with the Philippine people."

"Thank you," I replied. "And it is nice of you to be here to support a friend. Tell me about it."

"My friend works at Mary Kay's headquarters," she said.

She was a woman in her early 40s and dressed in a business suit. "What kind of work do you do?" I found out that she had a successful career in banking.

"I'm pleased to meet you. I'm Barbara Sunden."

"I'm Remedios, but everyone calls me Med," she said. We talked, and she explained, "I've been in banking for a while, and I like it. But I am curious. Can you tell me about becoming a Mary Kay consultant, and more about joining the company?"

I answered her questions and emphasized the opportunity we offered to women.

"I had never thought about doing anything like this, but you seem like somebody I would like to work with." She added, "I am impressed with how your company is so people-focused."

I talked about our company culture and how we were in the business of providing opportunities to women. "We need a company like yours in the Philippines," she answered. "I am sure your company will do very well here."

"I agree, Med," I said, "because we can offer them a better way of life." I then added, "Three days from now, we're having a training program. Why don't you come and learn more about what we do?"

She was very curious and agreed to come. As a successful businesswoman, she did some research on Mary Kay Inc. and said to me, "The company is sound financially, and it has an excellent reputation."

A short time after joining our company, Med left banking and quickly moved up the Mary Kay career path. During the next 12 months I made eight trips to the Philippines, and during this time I worked closely with her. I felt personally responsible for her success, and indeed, she became one of our top achievers. She left a high-level banking job to join our company. I knew that she didn't join our organization to conduct skin-care classes. With her background, she was looking at the big picture. Like I did when I came back after my son was born. I have always believed that one good leader can get many others to follow her. This is why I have focused on working with leaders. And my goodness, it makes it so much easier to build a sales organization when you go after individuals with leadership qualities.

Like I knew she would, Med reached out to a lot of people, and as a result, I have 60 directors and thousands of people in the Philippines. How did it happen? She heard me say a few words, and we connected. Some people might attribute this to luck, but I think it's intentioned. I believe that when you have an intention to go out and help people, the right relationship connects and good things happen.

It is also about thinking in terms of what's good for the other person. Sure, I am a businessperson, and I pay attention to the bottom line. But before I look at what I am going to get back, I always look at the value I can bring to others. When you think, "Wow, I've got something great to share," that's when you come across the opportunities that are out there.

At the end of my many trips to the Philippines, I was at the airport waiting for my flight back home. I met a Korean businessman who was waiting for his return flight to Korea, and we started to talk. He was curious about why so many American women had come to the Philippines without their husbands. I told him about what we do, and he asked for some literature about the company. I gave him a brochure.

"Do you do business in Korea?" he asked.

"We will soon. We are opening there after the first of the year."

"From what you say, it will be a wonderful opportunity for women in Korea, and I can introduce you to a lot of people," he said. He reached into his pocket and handed a business card to me. "Please give me your card." I did, he studied it briefly and said, "I will send you a list of women in Korea who I think will love to be invited to this opening."

I thanked him for his interest but didn't expect to ever hear from him. But when he sent three pages of faxes with women's names and addresses, I contacted him and said I'd come. So again, like in Canada and the Philippines, on a chance meeting with a stranger, I was on my way to Korea. While I was there, I recruited someone who is now one of the top achievers in Korea.

I've met so many others like these three examples in Canada, the Philippines, and Korea that I don't think of it as chance, which is another way of attributing it to luck. I think it has more to do with my gut reaction to people, which is a woman's intuition. I certainly don't have a patent on woman's intuition—most women have it. I, for one, happen to have a lot of faith in it. When I meet people and something inside tells me to learn more about them and figure out what value I can offer them, that's exactly what I do. I think women are more apt to have this intuition than men. It's something innate. It's "God's gift to women."

I know a woman's intuition is an intangible quality, and you can't put your arms around it. Just the same, it's worked for me so many times that I go with it. Is it 100 percent accurate? Of course it isn't. But it's worked for me so often that I believe in it.

⋆ Barry's and Bob's Comments ⋆

Barbara Sunden has had too much success throughout her long career to not take seriously what she says about her gut feelings and woman's intuition. Remember, she's the most successful person ever in an organization with more than 2 million current sales representatives. And with the millions of others who have sold Mary Kay products since its beginning in 1963, Barbara is the best ever of its past and present beauty consultants and sales directors. When an individual stands above a crowd of millions, it's foolhardy to credit luck and chance to the success she's enjoyed for such a long time.

As Barbara aptly describes her success, she relies on her intuition and calls it a gift from God. We agree that women are more in tune with other people's feelings and are better at reading them than men. But there are some women such as Barbara who seem to have mastered it, and as a result, as she puts it, they can connect with other people. To some, this sounds like mental telepathy, but we believe in it, too. As a seasoned salesperson knows, when you think in terms of what's best for your customer, he or she picks up signals and "connects" with you. The reverse is true—when you think solely of your self-interests, your customers pick up on that, too.

Barbara believes that women have this intuition. But obviously, not all are as gifted as others. However, like others in any field—a gifted artist, athlete, or entertainer—it takes hard work and practice to develop one's innate talent. Barbara's talent at connecting with others might have come naturally, but through experience and reflection, she fine-tuned it and over time grew to rely on it.

Selling What the End User Wants

Neil Friedman

President, Toys "R" Us

★ ★ ★

Neil Friedman is one of the most knowledgeable and respected executives in the toy business. Considered a toy industry icon, Friedman was named President of Toys "R" Us, U.S. in April 2011. Toys "R" Us has more than 879 stores as well as a highly successful online business in the U.S. Prior to joining the company, he had worked at Mattel since 1997 in a variety of executive roles, including serving as President of Mattel Brands. Friedman led the team credited for reinvigorating the Barbie brand. Just prior to working at Mattel, Friedman was President of Tyco PreSchool, owned by Tyco Industries, one of the world's largest toy manufacturers. He has held a number of other *key executive positions in the toy and juvenile products industries, including: President, MCA/Universal Merchandising; Senior Vice President, Sales, Marketing and Design, Just Toys; Vice President and General Manager, Baby Care, Gerber Products; Executive Vice President and Chief Operating Officer, Lionel Leisure Inc.; and President, Aviva/Hasbro.*

In 2004, Friedman was named to the Toy Industry Hall of Fame and inducted into the International Hall of Fame in 2007. He is a member of the board of trustees for the Toy Industry Foundation, and a lifetime advisor to the board of the Licensing Industry Merchandisers' Association. He serves on the executive advisory board for Children Affected by AIDS Foundation and is a member of the board of directors for both the New York Society for the Prevention of Cruelty to Children and the Northside Center for Child Development in New York City. He also serves on the board of directors of the Toys "R" Us Children's Fund.

Friedman holds a bachelor's degree in finance from Rider University in Lawrenceville, New Jersey.

★ ★ ★

It is hard to predict what toys children will like. No one bats 1,000 percent in this business.

When you sell a new toy concept internally to your people, the sale starts with you being sold on it. You won't come across as believable unless you believe that you have a winner.

As president of Toys "R" Us in the U.S.A., I'm now on the retail side of the toy business. However, I spent most of my career working for toy manufacturers. My story dates back to 1995 when I was president of Tyco Preschool, a division of Tyco Toys, and we were about to introduce a brand-new toy. That toy was Tickle Me Elmo, based on the Muppet from the popular TV show *Sesame Street*. In retrospect, one might think, "If there ever was a sure thing, it would have been Tickle Me Elmo." But in this business there are many more losers than winners, so there is never a sure thing.

The product was originally presented in 1994 as a toy monkey with a computer chip that laughed when it was squeezed. It was called Tickles the Chimp. At the time, Tyco wasn't licensed to make Sesame Street products, but we did have Looney Tunes rights. So we named it Tickle Me Taz but never brought it to the market. Later Tyco picked up the rights for Sesame Street. In 1995 we redesigned the toy, and it became Tickle Me Elmo, a mechanical doll with a computer chip that when squeezed would laugh. When tickled a second time, it laughed harder. When tickled a third time, Elmo would shake and laugh hysterically. It was that third squeeze that caught you by surprise, and that's what made children laugh and want to keep squeezing it.

My team and I met with a group of Tyco executives to get their approval on Elmo so we could get advertising dollars for a national campaign. We tested a storyboard for a TV commercial. If you've never seen one, a storyboard has drawings, panel by panel, much like a comic book. This is generally how we presented a commercial for a toy we felt had a lot of potential. When we made our presentation, the reaction by the Tyco executives was at best lukewarm, even though the test results met our standard for a commercial.

I was really excited about Elmo, but the decision makers whose approval we needed for the advertising dollars weren't enthused. "We're sorry, Neil, but we don't share your enthusiasm for this toy," one of them said.

"I hear you, and I know where you're coming from," I replied. "Elmo is a soft piece of plush. It's the kind of toy you've got to feel. People have to touch it, and they have to see how it works. I agree with you that looking at a soft toy on a storyboard does not tell its story."

They didn't say anything, and I continued, "There is something that I think is worth noting about the research that's been done on this Elmo commercial. The scores aren't acceptable, and considering the nature of this toy, we think this is a product that has to be touched. I feel this indicates that there is something special about Elmo."

Again, they remained silent and waited to hear where I was going.

"We will use a 'try-me package' so when shoppers are in the store, they can pick it up, feel it, and give it a squeeze," I continued. "In the try-me mode, the customers will get the surprise."

They seemed to be in doubt, so I added, "Don't you see that this is a wonderful interactive toy? It will retail for $29.99, which may be high for a soft toy, but there really aren't many soft toys at this price point that are interactive. Barney has proven that price point sells."

It was agreed to move forward with Elmo, and we got the advertising dollars needed to run with it. It was high enough to do the job, particularly for a soft toy with a $29.99 price tag. We were taking a big risk, and like I said, there are no sure things in this business. To our good fortune, Tickle Me Elmo was a home run. In 1996, stories were reported about parents who were literally fighting with other parents in stores to purchase Elmo for Christmas. The demand was so high that there were reports of Elmo owners selling him for as high as $1,500 on eBay. It was the nation's number-one selling toy in both 1996 and 1997. Ultimately, Tickle Me Elmo was *the* toy of the 1990s.

⋆ Barry's and Bob's Comments ⋆

It has been said that "nothing happens until a sale is made," and how well Neil Friedman knew this when he was seeking advertising dollars from Tyco executives to promote Tickle Me Elmo. An expert in his field, Friedman instinctively knew Elmo had potential to be a major toy, but he also understood that he had to sell it. The product wouldn't sell itself. Most importantly, he believed in what he was selling, and consequently, when the committee's first reaction was negative, he continued to present reasons why it should reconsider its initial opinion. By sticking to his convictions, he convinced it to commit to the advertising budget he requested to launch Tickle Me Elmo.

SUCCESS SECRETS OF SALES SUPERSTARS

Another lesson to learn from Friedman's story is that it is not what a company buyer thinks about the merits of product that's most important. Ultimately it is what the actual user will think about it. Friedman's success in this story was based on his ability to convince the executives that children would be enamored by Elmo because it was a fun toy and, as a kicker, the toy had a surprise when it was squeezed a third time. Ultimately, children loved Elmo, and they put pressure on their parents to buy one for them. Think about it: When parents asked their children what they wanted for Christmas, the response was, "I want Tickle Me Elmo!" And that's exactly what millions of children found under their Christmas trees in 1996–1997. Tickle Me Elmo went on to be one of the most successful toys of all time.

14 / Friedman: Selling What the End User Wants

Being a
Good Listener

Kirwan Elmers

Co-Founder, Custom Coach Corporation™

★ ★ ★

*I*n 1955 Kirwan Elmers co-founded Custom Coach Corporation *with his father, Miles Elmers. Based in Columbus, Ohio, it was the first American company to commercially offer custom motor-home conversions of bus shells. The company makes high-end custom motor homes for families, celebrities, and companies that sell as high as $1.5 million. Commercial units are built for special uses such as police command centers, computer labs, and mobile medical units.*

Over the years Elmers has personally sold custom coaches to many celebrities, including Clint Eastwood, Paul Newman, John Madden, Muhammad Ali, Chubby Checker, Evel Knievel, Roger

Penske, Dolly Parton, Johnny Cash, Ray Charles, George Foreman, The Emir of Kuwait, and the Saudi Arabian royal family. In 2002 Custom Coach™ became a division of Farber Specialty Vehicles, also based in Columbus. Elmers continues to work at Custom Coach.

★ ★ ★

Several years ago, I received a phone call from a man who lived in Cincinnati who asked a lot of questions about custom coaches. Interestingly, Cincinnati, which is a little over 100 miles south of Columbus, is a hub for motor coach owners. That's because it's home to the national headquarters of the Family Motor Coach Association, a trade association with thousands of registered owners of motor coaches of all sizes, small and large. The FMCA also hosts several trade shows every year, including some in other cities across the country. With the trade shows and publicity that the association generates, there are many motor coach owners residing in the area. For this reason, when I get an inquiry from someone in Cincinnati, I know that person is a good prospective buyer. Of course, when you've been in this business as long as I have, you get pretty good at knowing from a brief conversation who is genuinely interested in buying a motor coach. I could tell from the astute questions this man asked that he was.

After a lengthy conversation, the man said, "Thank you, Mr. Elmers, for your time and courtesy. In a few months from now, I'll be calling you about coming up to Columbus to see you with my wife."

"I look forward to it," I replied.

Sure enough, four months later, in early January, he called to set up an appointment with me so they could look at some custom coaches.

The couple's two sons, ages 10 and 12, accompanied them and so did their dog, a big Labrador. Generally when people bring the kids, it is a good sign that they are serious shoppers. And from my point of view, I love having children come. That's because children love motor homes. In fact, I can't imagine any child who wouldn't want his family to own one.

It was a beautiful, sunny day, and I showed them a dozen or so coaches. "Let's go inside," I said, and they followed me to a large conference table where we sat down. Then I noticed that only one boy was with us.

"Where's your other son?" I asked.

"We didn't want to leave the dog by himself in the van because he gets so lonely," the wife said. "Our son is in the van with him."

"Well, let's have the boy and the dog come inside."

"No, we can't bring our dog in your conference room," she said. "But thanks for the suggestion."

"We're all dog lovers around here," I said, "so let's go get the dog."

We all went out and got the other boy and brought him and the dog in. It was a well-behaved dog, and he curled up underneath the table. We then talked about what coach they should buy.

I listened to them tell me about how they wanted to do a lot of traveling with their two boys and take the dog along too. The husband was a consultant and had his office in their home. They owned two other homes. Their main residence was in Cincinnati, and they owned a home in upper-Michigan and another in Arizona. "I could work anywhere," he explained, "and when we travel to our other homes, each has an office for me. With a custom coach, we could travel all over the country, and I'd be able to get work done while we were on the road."

"We'd like to do some extensive traveling with the boys, and with a custom coach, I could home-school them," she enthusiastically explained.

"Yes, that would work," I said, "and what a great experience for your two boys."

"Yes, I can envision having a blackboard and some desks in the back," she said, thinking out loud about how she planned to custom their coach to fit their needs.

"And when my wife is driving," the husband added, "I could have my own workplace."

"It is a safe way to travel, isn't it?" she said.

"Due to its height, weight, and size, it's an extremely comfortable way to go," I said. "And yes, ma'am, it's also the safest way to travel. I want you to know that over the years with all the coaches we have on the road, some have been in accidents, but we've never had anyone in one of them killed or seriously injured. Interestingly, we built some coaches for McDonald's, and a while back another car went over a divider in downtown Chicago and hit their coach head-on. Some of the company's board members were in it, and no one was injured. One of them told me that had they been in a limousine somebody might have been killed or badly injured. Because the McDonald's people felt so safe, they said that's what influenced their decision to buy more coaches from us."

They were satisfied that owning a coach would be a safe way for their family to travel across the country. They talked a lot about how it would be a wonderful way for the boys to be schooled by mom. And dad could also stay on top of his consulting business with his "office on wheels." The woman asked some questions pertaining to how they would like to custom-make their coach to serve their needs, and I answered them.

At the point when I thought it was time to close the sale, I said, "You will need to put down a $25,000 deposit on the coach shell and another $25,000 for a deposit on the interior work. Then we'll get your drawing started and be on our way."

The wife took out her checkbook and wrote a check for $50,000. "Okay, let's get that out of the way," she said, and handed the check to me.

"Okay," I said, "let's talk about how we're going to build your coach."

⋆ Barry's and Bob's Comments ⋆

It is interesting how Elmers asked the couple to bring in their dog and son who were waiting in the family van. "I tell people that I sold that coach to the dog," he jokes. "Of course the dog didn't buy the coach, but it certainly helped to have it there." It did for three reasons. First, had the boy and dog stayed in the van, the couple would have been apprehensive about leaving them alone, which would have been distracting. Second, it could have caused them to rush through the sales presentation, and had that happened, there might not have been sufficient time for Elmers to close the sale. Third, dog lovers trust other dog lovers. The fact that Elmers was also a dog lover sent a message to the couple that he was trustworthy. Certainly, one could say that being a dog lover or claiming to be a dog lover has little or nothing to do with one's honesty. And if you are from that school of thought, we won't argue with you. However, we do believe that people's emotions do influence their buying decisions. With this in mind, we tend to believe that Elmers' response to the dog was to some degree a difference maker.

On another subject, Elmers explains that every custom coach is different and therefore no sales presentation is alike because it must cater to different people's needs. We stress that when you sell a product such as a custom coach, you have to be a good listener; otherwise, you might never know what your customer wants.

Doing Good Is Good for Business

Rob Groeschen

Founder, CEO, Resource One and InRETURN

★ ★ ★

Rob Groeschen is the founder and CEO of Resource One, a privately held environmental recycling company based in Cincinnati, Ohio, that provides innovative recycling and reuse programs. Resource One offers services that assist companies in reducing environmental regulation exposure and eliminating hazardous waste. Resource One's customers include small, medium, and large companies and include Honda, Sherwin-Williams, and Whirlpool.

Born and raised in Fort Thomas, Kentucky, just across the Ohio River from Cincinnati, Rob graduated from Eastern Kentucky University in 1987 and moved to Orlando, Florida, where he took *a job driving a hazardous-waste truck as a route service representative for Safety-Kleen, an environmental service company. In 1991, Groeschen was transferred to Cincinnati, where he assumed managerial responsibilities. In 1999, he ventured out on his own, forming Resource One. In 2010 Resource One was named Honda Supplier of the Year. In 2012, its revenues were $12 million.*

In 2004, Groeschen formed InRETURN, a nonprofit organization housed in a warehouse-and-office facility adjacent to Resource One. The new enterprise was incorporated under the Internal Revenue Code tax exemption Section 501 (c) (3). InRETURN offers employment opportunities to individuals who have suffered a neurological injury, disease, or disorder.

★ ★ ★

Our father passed away when I was 11, so my big brother Tom, 13, was my role model. He was a standout athlete and a good student. During his senior year in high school, Tom was Kentucky's All-State first-team running back and the school's homecoming and prom king. Handsome, with a winning personality, everyone loved Tom. I was his biggest fan. He was my hero. I was an underachiever, and I basked in my big brother's glory. When he went away to college, I didn't know how I'd live without being around him. I couldn't wait to finish my senior year so I could join him at Eastern in Richmond, Kentucky.

On the night of August 10, 1983, my brother was in a terrible automobile accident that drastically changed his life forever. In retrospect, my life was also forever changed. At age 19, Tom was almost killed in a crash on Interstate 471. He suffered severe head trauma, a collapsed lung, and his heart stopped for a short period. He was in and out of a coma for more than three months and the doctors prepared our family for the worst. My brother survived but would never again be the old Tom—the handsome star athlete who oozed charm. Tom was unable to attend school, and with his brain injuries, the physicians said that he would be acutely impaired for the rest of his life.

Until this point in my life, Tom had always looked after me. When we were kids playing ball in the sandlot, he was always the captain, and during pickup games, had he not picked me, I would have been the last kid picked. He always looked after me. I thought he was the world's best big brother. After the accident, I knew that from that point on, our roles would be reversed. It would now be my turn to look after Tom, and I made a vow that I would always be there for him. Had it not been for that commitment, it is doubtful that I would have started my own company. I did it because I wanted to make sure Tom always had a job, and I knew that as long as I was self-employed, there would be a place for him. Before I started Resource One, Tom had a job cleaning bathrooms at a rest stop on Interstate 75 in northern Kentucky. He was paid a minimum wage of $7 an hour and had to leave our home at 5 A.M. on a two-hour bus ride that required transfers. After work he endured another two-hour return bus ride. He kept that job for nearly 10 years, but it did little for his self-esteem. Whenever someone asked him what kind of work he did, he'd say, "I clean toilets for a living, and I pick up other people's shit." I hated that and always told him, "Why can't you just say you work for the highway department?"

When I started Resource One, I made sure there was always a place for Tom to work. When I saw how he thrived on having responsibility, I decided I would someday start an organization that employed others with similar impairments, so like Tom, they could also be gainfully employed and develop self-respect. After being on my own for five years, I started InRETURN, a company dedicated to hiring handicapped people like Tom. Over the years, it's become more than just a place of employment. In addition to having a normal work environment, our production associates, as they are called, have 10-minute breaks each hour; during these periods and on their lunch hour, they can watch TV, play cards, shoot pool, and just hang out with each other. From 2 to 3 P.M. we have daily life skills classes that include handwriting sessions, book clubs, cooking lessons, art projects, and even dance lessons. We have a van that takes associates to and from work.

Initially I set up InRETURN as a workplace for my brother and others like him, but it evolved into something much bigger and now employs 16 production associates. As Resource One grows, it will grow.

InRETURN was never intended as a tool to generate sales for Resource One. After all, business is business, and the high-quality service we offer is what we sell and what generates repeat orders. If we didn't offer more bang for the buck, we wouldn't be able to compete in the highly competitive recycling industry. Of course, it also takes good old-fashioned persistence to open new accounts, and that's no easy matter for a small company when it comes to getting a foot in the door with a giant international company like Honda Manufacturing Company. I vividly remember getting up my nerve to make my first call on Shaun Stepp, who at the time was the engineer coordinator of its facilities department, handling utility supplies for its massive plant in Marysville, Ohio. Shaun turned me down seven times before I got an order. It was a relatively small order from such a large company, only $500 a month for its absorbent program, which involved placing pads around the base of compressors to soak up the oil. We picked up these pads and sent them out to be laundered. I think I finally got the business because I wore Shaun down. But once we had the business, we worked overtime to show Honda how good we were.

I remember one time when I came down with a case of pneumonia and was so sick my wife had to drive me to the Marysville plant so I could keep an appointment with Shaun. I slept in the back of the car while she drove the 240-mile round trip. When Shaun saw me, he said, "Rob, you look terrible. You're as sick as a dog. What are you doing out of bed?" I wanted him to know that we valued Honda's business and were dedicated to serving the company. Gradually we picked up more business from them, eventually running around $2,000 a month. There was so much potential for more business at the Honda site, but they kept telling me that we were too small a company. Companies like Waste Management and Ashland Chemical Company were getting the lion's share of their business. Although I tried to convince Shaun that we should get a shot at helping Honda incorporate better ways to recycle and reuse waste materials, we were viewed as a small player, which meant we'd only get small jobs in comparison to what the big players got.

Meanwhile, Shaun and I developed a rapport and every now and then we played a round of golf. A turning point occurred when I invited him to an InRETURN fundraising golf outing. Shawn came down to Cincinnati with his golf clubs, but while in town, he visited our plant.

When Shaun saw our production associates at work and learned about our rehabilitation program, he said, "How cool is this? How come you never told me about this before? I had no idea that you were doing this."

Having seen the production associates in action and realizing how much their jobs meant to them, Shaun became emotionally involved. When he realized that our production associates worked on an assembly line that made absorbent socks, he said, "We should be using yours." Until that point, we were just picking up waste materials—we weren't supplying Honda with any absorbents. By making them, picking them up, and recycling them, the volume of business substantially increased. It was a win-win because ours did a better job at absorbing oils and coolants then the previous ones they used. Additionally, ours were more effective at reducing spill hazards and slip hazards. Then, once the socks were saturated, we found sources that used them as fuel in a recycling program. Consequently, we provided a more environment-friendly solution.

"I always enjoyed working with you, Rob," Shaun told me. "Now seeing what you do at InRETURN and knowing how much you care and give so much back, it's a privilege working with your company."

Shaun was transferred to another area at the Marysville plant, and I started dealing with his boss, Buck Winterhoff, who increased the amount of work we did for Honda. In 2010, we received a Supplier of the Year Award from Honda, and Buck and three executives, including Dirk Nordberg, Buck's boss, came to visit our plant. They wanted to see what we do, and they wanted to talk to our administrative people. During a tour of our site, they spent time talking to our production associates and observed the activities we had for them during their breaks and the daily classes. They also met my brother Tom and learned about my personal motivation for wanting to start InRETURN. Prior to their visit, some of them didn't know about InRETURN. It was a real eye-opener for them.

One of them asked me, "Why didn't you tell me you did this?"

"I didn't think it was fair game," I answered. "It has never been my intention to use InRETURN as a marketing tool, and it still isn't. It may get discovered through audits of our company and by tours of our facility, and yes, it is who we are and what we do. But we understand that we're in a competitive business, and the success of Resource One is dependent on showing our customers a better way. If we don't, we will be replaced by another company."

"Business is about relationships," Buck Winterhoff said to me, "and there is a trust factor that we think is important at Honda. We also value who you and your people are as individuals. We talk a lot about family values at Honda, and we can see by your actions that family means a lot to you. This is clear by what you do at InRETURN and how your inspiration came out of your love for your brother. This tells us a lot about who you are. I also like the way you are making a difference in other people's lives."

Dirk Nordberg pulled me aside and said, "I just want to personally thank you, Rob, for what you guys do here. You are doing a great job."

Evidently, my brother, Tom, must have made a good impression on them because whenever I see these executives at their site, they ask about him. They'll often say something like: "Give your brother my regards," or "How's Tom doing?"

Our business has steadily increased with Honda, and today, we have 17 of our people working at the site in Marysville. As its sole supplier, we manage all its recycle materials from start to finish, which is about $1.8 million annually.

✶ Barry's and Bob's Comments ✶

In basketball, it's said that the home court has a six-point advantage. In business, it's also an advantage to have customers visit your facility to learn more about you. By getting to know your people (vs. only you, a sales rep), they observe that you are more than a one-man show—you are part of a team. It's good for them to realize that there are others there to serve them, and it's beneficial to them to have contact with your co-workers. With this in mind, even without InRETURN, Groeschen would have benefited from Honda's visit to his plant. As an added bonus, Groeschen's customers who visit InRETURN become privy to the incredibly good deeds he does, which makes them want to do business with his company.

You can be rewarded in the same way. A 2010 survey by America's Research Group stated that 81 percent of American consumers claimed they are more loyal to a company that is active in the community. The same survey revealed that 95 percent of American employees boast about their bosses' civic activities and it makes them feel proud to work for the company. ARG's research confirms that doing good deeds is good business—and it's the right thing to do.

Knowledge—There Is No Substitute for It!

Jeffrey S. Schottenstein

Merrill Lynch Managing Director—Investments; Private Wealth Advisor

*J*eff Schottenstein is considered one of the top private wealth advisors in the United States. In 1995 at age 26, after receiving an MBA in finance from the Kellogg Graduate School of Management at Northwestern University, he began his career with the Montgomery Securities Private Client Department in San Francisco. In 2002, Schottenstein and his team joined the Merrill Lynch Private Banking & Investment Group, where they continue to provide comprehensive wealth management to a high-net-worth clientele.

Jeff has been recognized by Barron's and other sources as one of the nation's top financial advisors. In 2005 and again in 2006, he was ranked as Merrill Lynch's number-one financial advisor based on revenue produced. In 2006 and 2007, the Barron's *list of the top 100 financial advisors in America ranked Schottenstein 12 and 15, respectively. He is active in the San Francisco community and serves on the board of First Graduate, an organization helping young people finish high school and become the first in their family to graduate from college.*

★ ★ ★

Upon earning my MBA, I moved to San Francisco and joined Montgomery Securities, a prestigious boutique investment firm that specialized in catering to high-net-worth clients. I had previously worked as a sales representative selling carpet for Shaw Industries while attending night school at Northwestern's business school. My fellow Private Client Department trainees had pedigreed backgrounds from fine schools such as Harvard and Stanford; some came with Wall Street experience. I was the only carpet salesman in my training class. We were told at the start that no matter how educated and accomplished we were, our performance would determine who would survive in the highly competitive investment industry. It was a business that was tangibly results-oriented. While I was filled with anxiety, it was comforting to always know where I stood.

I planned to rely on a personal formula for success that always gave me an edge over others in previous endeavors. I was counting on my strong work ethic to help me rise to the top. I was willing to outwork everyone else and put in as many hours and make as many calls as it took in order to succeed. Sure, I knew I lacked knowledge and experience, but by getting in at five in the morning and leaving late at night and by working weekends, I knew I'd do well. I understood that was the price I'd have to pay as a rookie in the business, and I was more than willing to ante up.

As a member of Montgomery's Private Client Department, I planned to pursue individuals with immense wealth. This meant I would seek out clients who were CEOs, venture capitalists, and founders of companies engaged in public offerings or being sold. As a novice, it was difficult to get my foot in the door.

In 1997, Montgomery's bankers were participating in a secondary offering for a fast-growing public company based on the East Coast. Coincidentally, a while back, I had met the company's dynamic young CEO, who was a friend of a friend of a friend. At this stage in my fledgling career, I had made countless calls to wealthy prospects, but rarely did anyone get back to me. Knowing that we had once met, my supervisor said, "Go ahead, Jeff, give him a call."

Not certain if this busy executive would even know who I was, I mustered up the nerve to call him. I left a message with his assistant, and to my amazement, he returned my call. I could hardly believe it. He couldn't have been more receptive. When I suggested that I fly to the East Coast so we could meet for a drink, he said, "By all means, Jeff. I'd be happy to see you."

I remember how hopeful I felt that somebody this important had consented to meet with me. Being a boutique firm with only one office in San Francisco, Montgomery often supported its salespeople by paying their travel expenses to meet with worthy prospects across the country. The company agreed to pick up the tab, and I jumped on a plane to the East Coast. At this point in my career, I had developed a sales presentation that explained my investment philosophy. I was good at articulating the story of Montgomery. I understood the importance of asset allocation and the implementation of a strategy. Plus, I could explain why you don't time the market, and so on. I had my uniform on—suit, cufflinks, and shined shoes. I was ready. At least I thought I was.

In the beginning, we chatted over a drink. I explained how our firm provided comprehensive wealth management to CEOs of public companies, and I emphasized that our services included diversification and hedging strategies for a restricted equity position in an insider's own company. So far, so good.

Then the CEO began to ask me some incredibly detailed questions about restricted equity. I knew that CEOs and insiders had to comply with specific securities laws and regulations when buying and selling their company stock. I was familiar with the fact that there were multiple forms to file, and I realized that there were certain windows pertaining to when an insider could transact. It is fairly complex, and while I had a basic understanding of this world, along with the backup of experts within our firm, I was not equipped to handle all the CEO's questions. He was so intelligent and inherently curious that the more he probed into the details, the more I realized how ill-equipped I was to answer his questions.

"How are variable pre-paid forward transactions constructed?" he asked.

"What's the lockup and fees for your exchange funds?"

"What about short-swing-profit rules?"

"Rule 144?"

"Section 16?"

"Charitable remainder trusts?"

I felt blood rush to my head. I wasn't able to completely answer these questions, and I kept thinking to myself, "Jeff, you are blowing it."

I realized I was in completely over my head. I simply lacked the knowledge required to do the job at hand. My firm had incurred the expense for me to travel across the country. And there I was. I was able to get this CEO to give me his scarce time, and that by itself was a major personal accomplishment back then. It crossed my mind that I had made thousands of calls in order to actually have an opportunity like this. And now I couldn't answer these direct questions. I was so mad at myself. It was totally unacceptable. All I could think was, "Jeff, you're all cufflinks and no content."

The only good thing I did was remember from my training class at Shaw Industries, "If you don't know the answer, don't dance around. Instead you say, 'I don't know, but I will find out and get back to you.'" While I loathed repeatedly saying that, I had no choice. I knew it was better than dancing. Meanwhile in the back of my mind, my biggest fear was that I would never get a second opportunity to come back with the answers to his questions.

The trip home was a real downer. But I resolved to master this content as well as other areas of content in my profession. I was determined to really learn this stuff. Completely—once and for all. I wanted to become a true expert in my field. I expanded my business strategy from being the individual who made the most calls to also being the one who was equipped with the deepest portfolio of knowledge. I understood that nothing in the business was so complicated that I couldn't master it. Yes, a lot of it was dry and somewhat boring, but it was totally learnable, and I would learn it.

I studied day and night, and a month later, I called the CEO to request another meeting with him. He graciously agreed to meet me for breakfast, and again I flew back East. This time I was fully prepared and committed to never again waste his time. We met, and again he fired questions at me, but this time, I comfortably, eagerly, and enjoyably took him through every aspect in detail of restricted stock strategies. There wasn't a single question I didn't fully answer.

I loved it. I wasn't selling. I was teaching. For that full hour we spent together, I had become the trusted advisor to a CEO. Imagine that, I thought to myself—not at all bad for an ex-carpet salesman!

By the CEO's reaction, I could see that he was pleased that he'd given me a second opportunity and I didn't let him down. I left the meeting feeling quite proud of myself, and I knew right there and then that this would be the approach to the business that I would follow from that day forward. I would rely on substance to win customers and their loyalty. I wasn't going to depend on wining, dining, and charming people. My future success would be based on my ability to educate and serve clients.

In the months that followed, this gentleman opened an account with me and sent in a block of stock. Over the years, he has referred me to his partners, executives, family members, and founders of other companies that his company acquired. We've carefully traded millions of his company's shares, and we've provided ongoing reinvestment services. Over the past 14 years that I've been associated with him and his family, we've developed a meaningful friendship. Recently we had dinner together, and I thanked him for everything he has done for me. I wanted to make sure he knew how important a role he's played in my career. A humble man, he simply smiled.

☆ Barry's and Bob's Comments ☆

As Jeff Schottenstein's story emphasizes, there is no substitute for knowledge. In our opinion, no business is so complicated that one could have an excuse for not being an expert in her or his field. Of course, we all know that most people do lack expertise in their business. It boils down to pure laziness. Few are willing to pay the price of success by learning what they need to know to properly serve their customers. Not only is it unprofessional, it's a sign of disrespect for a customer's time. When people are willing to take the time to seek your services vs. your competitor's, you should feel obligated to know your business backward and forward so you don't waste their valuable time. Anything less is unprofessional and unacceptable.

Selling Homes to the Rich and Famous

Joyce Rey

America's Legendary Residential Real Estate Salesperson

★ ★ ★

ased in Beverly Hills, California, Joyce Rey has sold more high-priced residential properties than any other individual in the U.S. She is currently one of only two executive directors of Previews International, the Estates Division of Coldwell Banker, in the United States. Rey began her career in 1973; six years later she organized the original and legendary Rodeo Realty, the first real estate firm to exclusively represent $1 million-plus properties. In 2010 Joyce listed and closed a $72 million property, the highest-priced residential transaction in the United States that year.

In 2009 Haute Living selected Rey as one of the 100 most influential Angeleños. The National Women's Political

Committee named her "Miss October" in its 2008 calendar of women leaders in California. The Los Angeles Times *presented her with its Global Image Leader Award in 2008, and that same year, the American Cancer Society honored Rey with its Spirit of Life Award. In 2006,* Unique Homes *magazine selected Rey as one of America's 35 Most Influential People in luxury real estate and presented her with its Award of Excellence. She was selected because she represents the most exclusive homes in the country as well as for her extensive community involvement. In the 1990s, she received the Pinnacle Award, an honor given by her firm to the top ten residential real estate professionals in the U.S., four times. In 1991, Rey was named America's number-one agent by Prudential Real Estate Affiliates. A $30 million residential listing where she represented both the seller and the buyer was Bel Air's record high sale for the decade in the 1990s. Her impressive real estate career spans four decades and is heralded as the most successful ever in the exclusive residential homes field. Her list of clients includes the very rich and famous from around the world, including such faraway places as China, Japan, and Russia.*

I n 1976 I had only had my real estate license for three years when I sold a home owned by Sonny and Cher in Holmby Hills, an affluent neighborhood in west side Los Angeles bordered by Beverly Hills on the east and Bel Air on the north. The buyers wanted to buy an exclusive property that was the crème de la crème, and back then, paying $1 million for a home was a huge amount of money. It was my first million-dollar sale.

After living in the house for two years, the owners asked me to sell it. "Our asking price will be $2.5 million. We know that's an outrageous amount of money, but see if you can get it for us. We're leaving for Switzerland, but call us if you have an offer while we're gone."

"I'll try," I assured them, knowing that nobody had sold a house in that price range ever at that time.

"Oh, one more thing, Joyce," the husband said. "We don't want anybody to know that we're selling it. You can't put it in the multiple listing service, and we don't want you to advertise it."

I remembered that Rod Stewart, the talented entertainer, loved the house when Sonny and Cher occupied it. I called Rod to tell him that it was on the market, and he said, "Joyce, I want to see it immediately." I was excited about it and met him at the property. We toured the house. It looked fabulous. We went through the entire property, and Rod loved every bit of it.

It's funny how I remember little things from so long ago. I'll never forget that Rod was wearing red satin tennis shoes. I suppose in my business, one pays attention to small details. After we looked at everything, he said, "I'm willing to pay full price for this house."

Offering full price was astounding, especially because it was such a huge number in those days. I wrote up the offer and called the owners, who had arrived in Switzerland. "I'm so excited," I told them. "I have this full price offer for you. Do you realize how incredible that is? I have a buyer who will pay your asking price of $2.5 million! Rarely does anyone pay the full asking price for such an expensive home."

Their response was, "Joyce, what do you want first—the good news or the bad news?"

No one knew the house was for sale, and I had called one person and gotten an offer. How could there be any bad news? I had a full-price offer.

"There's bad news?" I asked.

"Joyce, the bad news is that we've been looking at properties here in Switzerland, and we've been considering buying a penthouse. They're getting over a million dollars for small apartments here. If this is what an apartment is worth, we think we've underpriced our house. We won't accept $2.5 million; now we want $4.5 million for it."

I was stunned. I didn't know of anyone who had paid $2 million for a house in the United States back then, and I had a $2.5 million offer in my hand.

They explained that their reason for wanting more money was because they were convinced that real estate was becoming a global market, and we'd soon see foreign demand for U.S. properties that we had not seen before. My clients believed that because they had been traveling abroad, they had a feel for what was going on in Europe and were ahead of the curve.

"Did you say something about some good news?" I asked.

"Yes, Joyce," the husband said. "We think you're terrific, and we're going to give you a two-year listing."

That was some consolation; typically back then, real estate agents were given only 90 days to sell a property. But clearly, I would have rather closed a $2.5 million deal where I was the listing and selling agent than a house that I might sell at an astronomically high price. As the adage goes, "A bird in the hand is worth two in the bush."

My next thought was, "What in the world am I going to tell Rod?" Of course, I told him the owners had changed their minds, and he was not happy at all. He dismissed the house, and there I was, sitting on a house that seemed way overpriced. But I had two years to sell it.

Six months later, I was sitting on a chaise lounge by the pool at the Beverly Hills Hotel with a foreign buyer from the Mideast. He was represented by another broker and wanted anonymity. He asked for my guidance to prepare his offer, which was $4 million for the property. We settled on $4.2 million.

Real estate in the U.S. did go global. Seven years ago the house with the neighboring property attached to it sold for just under $30 million. The sellers were right when they said they were ahead of the curve.

★ Barry's and Bob's Comments ★

Joyce Rey emphasizes that patience is an important virtue to a realtor. And she demonstrated considerable patience when her sellers turned down a $2.5 million offer that had matched their asking price. Other salespeople might have been angry, and their reaction would have been to express their displeasure to the homeowners for not accepting the price they'd agreed upon. We can only imagine the disappointment Rey must have felt when the sellers turned down $2.5 million, which would not only have been her biggest sale to date but her first multimillion-dollar sale! Had she gotten into a dispute with the sellers, she might have won the battle but lost the war.

Rather than taking a belligerent stance, she acted like a lady—Joyce Rey is a class act. Instead of crying foul, she willingly said that she would do whatever her clients desired. As our research revealed, Joyce Rey is a true professional and always looks out for the best interests of her many clients. How well she understands that her number-one priority is to serve her client. It's no wonder that, over the years, affluent people come to her when they want to sell or buy multimillion-dollar homes.

A Matter of Trust

Douglas Vlchek

Chief Wisdom Officer Emeritus/Senior Vice President DaVita Inc.

★ ★ ★

D oug Vlchek is known as "Yoda" throughout the village, where he and his 40,000-plus teammates work at DaVita, which owns and operates 1,777 kidney dialysis centers in 45 states, serving approximately 140,000 patients. A Fortune 500 company, DaVita is one of its industry's leaders in the U.S. Vlchek was the company's first chief wisdom officer from 1999 to 2006, retired, and came back again in 2009 to work part time. He is now chief wisdom officer emeritus as well as senior vice president. An ordained deacon in the Roman Catholic Church, during his absence, Vlchek was the director of stewardship at the Roman Catholic Diocese of Cheyenne, Wyoming.

Vlchek is credited for being one of the creators of DaVita's unique culture, known as "The DaVita Way." He was the architect of DaVita University, the company's personal and professional development program for all its employees, who are known as teammates.

Vlchek entered the dialysis industry in 1970. From 1985 to 1997 he owned and operated Douglas L. Vlchek & Associates, a consulting firm to providers of kidney dialysis services. In 1998 to 2000, he was vice president and chief knowledge officer of Vivra Asthma & Allergy, and in 1997 to 1998, he served as vice president of Gambro Healthcare. From 2004 to 2006, he served as director of religious education at Our Lady of the Mountains Catholic Church in Jackson, Wyoming. He has worked in the Catholic Church since 1985 and as a deacon since 1999, after five years of seminary education in Denver.

Vlchek graduated from Case Western Reserve University in 1971 with a B.A. in biology and did graduate study in biochemistry there from 1971 to 1972. He has served on numerous boards in the nephrology and hemodialysis fields and has received many awards in the health-care field. He has authored more than 200 articles, most of which are on dialysis and related subjects. He is the author of five books on the topics of quality assurance and continuous quality improvement in health care.

★ ★ ★

We have an unusual company culture at DaVita. The people who work here are "teammates," and we work in what we call a "village." Kent Thiry, our CEO, is known as the "Mayor" of the village. He and I worked together in the dialysis industry prior to my joining the company in late 1999. A short time afterward he introduced me to his management team at a meeting in January 2000 and never referred to me by my name. He called me "Yoda," and he kept saying, "Yoda did this and Yoda did that." He later let them know that he had been calling me that for years and that even his children call me Yoda. I'm not sure they even know my real name! The nickname comes from the movie *Star Wars,* in which Yoda was one of the most powerful Jedi Masters in galactic history, renowned for his legendary wisdom. Kent says that he learned a lot from me and that I teach deeper things beyond management principles or clinical issues. He knows that I teach folks about how to treat each other well. Kent insists that he's learned a great deal from me. While what he says is flattering, I think it is I who learned so much from him.

In 1999 the company, then called Total Renal Care, was on the verge of bankruptcy. The price of its stock had been as high as $50 but by March 1999 it had fallen to $2.06. The company was $1.5 billion in debt, defaulting on its loans and having trouble meeting its weekly payroll. Much of this was due to numerous problems with billing and collecting, but there were over a dozen other significant problems, including the government refusing to pay for laboratory tests, ill-advised ventures into other ancillary businesses, and a SEC investigation. Shareholder unrest distracted employees, so morale plummeted.

This was the scenario when Kent was hired as CEO in September 1999. He recruited me a few months later. Kent came with pedigree credentials. A Stanford grad with an MBA from Harvard, he was a partner at Bain & Company and had served as CEO for Vivra Renal Care, a dialysis chain based in Southern California. Kent brought in some senior people including Joe Mello, a mutual friend we both had worked with. Joe was hired as the company's chief operating officer. We knew that if we were going to turn the company around, we'd have to make major changes in the company's culture. That's no easy matter, and we had to do it while we were fixing our serious cash flow as well as other operational problems. To complicate matters, the company had 10,000-plus people who were scattered around the country working at 564 dialysis facilities serving more than 44,000 patients.

Part of my job was to implement "The DaVita Way," a philosophy that defines the culture we planned to create. Simply stated, the DaVita Way means that we dedicate our heads, hearts, and hands to pursue our mission, live the values, and build a healthy village. This means we care for each other with the same intensity with which we care for our patients. By the way, it's important that you know that "DaVita" is a loose translation of "to give life" in Italian.

To get things started, we had a management meeting with 650 teammates in attendance. After several days of conducting small group discussions, we asked everyone to vote on what should be our company's core values—those behavioral concepts upon which we could achieve alignment and to which we could hold each other accountable. Over several discussions, we came up with Service Excellence, Integrity, Team, Continuous Improvement, Accountability, and Fulfillment. A couple of years later, at the request of a majority of our teammates, "Fun" was added as our seventh core value.

Now, I realize that we are not unlike many other organizations that claim to have a mission and core values. What I believe is different about ours is that we actually recruit and hire based on alignment with those mission and values. When we evaluate teammates, we consider how they are doing at "living" the values to be just as important as their technical job performance. And we consider the highest honors within our "village" to be awards given to those who exemplify its values. Few meetings (even board meetings!) take place, even at the highest level when deciding questions worth tens of millions of dollars, without someone asking, "Is this consistent with our mission and values?" At DaVita, the mission and values are not just pretty words hanging on a poster in the corporate office. They are, literally, the framework and the common ground we use for working together and guiding our daily decision making.

At the same meeting at which we created the core values, it became clear that a lot of our teammates no longer wanted to be called Total Renal Care because that name was associated with some negative things that the company had been in the past. Choosing from a list of many names, we narrowed it down to three, and our teammates voted to change the company name to DaVita. As far as we know, that was the first time a Fortune 500 company had its people vote on naming it.

Now before I continue, here are a few things about me that are relevant to my story—events that occurred that shaped who I am today and affect what I have done with my career, particularly at DaVita. I'll start when I was growing up in inner-city Cleveland, Ohio. We did not have a lot of money (many might say we were poor); so for the first eight years of my life we lived in the house of my grandparents, who had immigrated to America from Poland and Austria. My grandfather worked the night shift in a steel mill, and, because my parents both worked full time, my grandfather took care of me during the day. I remember how he'd pull me around in a little red wagon when he went shopping and he'd stop to chat with neighbors. We were always together, and I learned so much from him. He, more than any other human being, formed me—taught me how to be a man. Among hundreds of important talks we had, I remember one day when he asked, "Doug, what do you want to be when you grow up?"

That was a serious question to ask a 4-year-old boy. "I'm not sure, Grandpa," I answered, "but I do know that when I grow up I want to do something good with my life . . . and Good with a capital 'G'!" And that was a serious answer for a 4-year-old.

I'll now fast-forward to the time when my family moved to a Cleveland suburban area. My parents were not churchgoing people, so during my formative years I had not spent much time in church. When I was 9, however, I do recall attending one church and seeing a big picture of St. Peter and Jesus. I can still see that picture in my mind to this very day. It depicted Peter, who had his fishing nets over his arm, and there was a boat in the background. Underneath the picture, a caption, recounting Jesus' words to Peter, read, "Follow me and I will make you a fisher of men."

For weeks I asked my parents to explain what it meant. "What's a fisher of men?" I insisted on knowing. They really never gave me a satisfactory answer, so I kept asking and saying, "I need to know."

Something inside me kept reminding me of the message on that picture. In retrospect, I now know with that picture and that caption, God was telling me what I was supposed to do with my life. That's right, at age 9 I began to understand what my life was supposed to be. I was going to be a "fisher of people." I would help people understand that there is a way we should live our lives. Yes, I began to be determined that's what I would do when I grew up.

Nine years later, I was 18, had graduated from high school and was getting ready to start college at Case Western Reserve University in Cleveland. My sister, who was a year younger than me, had a boyfriend, Ken, who was my best friend. One day, Ken came over with a black eye. He didn't say how he got it, but a mutual friend told me that Ken had been in a fistfight with some guys because one of them had called me a liar. I don't remember what the accusation was, but Ken was furious about it. He said, "Vlchek don't lie, and you take that back." (Ken's language was actually a little more colorful. I believe the exact words were "Vlchek don't talk no sh*t").

The fact that a teenage friend would defend my honor was quite humbling to me. And for the rest of my life I have tried to live up to always being truthful so Ken's beating would not have been in vain. To this day I think about this story, and sometimes tell it to DaVita teammates when I speak to them at Academy.

DaVita Academy is a year-round series of classes attended by DaVita teammates. The purposes of DaVita Academy are to provide personal and professional development, enhance teammate engagement, and to provide some tools associated with those purposes. We spend a significant amount of time showing teammates how they can actually "live" our mission and values on a day-to-day basis. Of course patient care is our first priority, but we believe it starts with caring for and growing our teammates. The Academy brings them together and allows teammates to learn about themselves and the DaVita Way. To date, over 20,000 DaVita teammates have "graduated" from the two-day Academy.

One of the "classes" that I helped design for the Academy asks teammates to think about their "personal credo" (a modified version of an exercise we learned from leadership guru Jim Kouzes, who wrote the book *Credibility*). In this exercise we ask them to develop a statement about what they really believe in, what is important to them, and what is important in their life. What they "stand for," and what they "won't stand for." I tell them about my own personal credo, which is:

☆ Love God, Be His Instrument
☆ Truth
☆ Do Good (Love, Servant Leadership)
☆ Family Before Self
☆ Discover→Experience→Learn→Teach
☆ Give It Everything ("leave nothing on the field")
☆ Be the Enemy of Fear
☆ Be Happy (see the best in everyone)

When I talk about that second point, Truth, I explain how the incident with my friend Ken has impacted my life.

I also talk about the DaVita Way and about serving our patients; and I remind them that caring for each other with the same intensity that we care for our patients is equally fundamental within DaVita. I think that's one of the things that sets us apart from most other health-care organizations. I actually tell them, "If you tell me you love your patients, but you don't really care very deeply for your co-workers, then you don't 'get' DaVita. Yes, you love your patients, I've clearly heard that from you," I say; and then I emphasize, "You need to love each other in the same way." "Love each other"—this is not something you'll hear from many senior vice presidents at Fortune 500 companies. But you do hear it said often at DaVita—and not just from me, but from many teammates at all levels throughout the organization—from caregivers to business office teammates from coast to coast, and even from other senior executives.

I am currently working on my master's degree in theology. One of the recurring themes in the Bible is about loving God. Jesus said, "The greatest commandment is this: You shall love the Lord, your God, with all your heart, with all your soul, and with all your mind." And the second commandment is like it: "You shall love your neighbor as yourself." It is my belief that those two "commandments" are integrally connected. How can you show you love God? You can't touch him. You can't see him. But you can love the creatures and people He created and put on this world with you. When we show our love for all of them, we are actually showing our love for God.

When I talk to our people about the DaVita Way, I always tell them, "It's absolutely incredible what we get to do for a living." I say, "The name of the company, 'DaVita,' actually defines what we do for a living. DaVita means 'To give life.' What we do for a living is 'give life.'" Then I pause and add, "I'm not just talking about caring for and keeping dialysis patients alive. I'm talking about what you do for each other. If you are truly showing love for each other, you are giving life to that person sitting next to you or working in the cubicle next to you. This is what we do for a living. That's what I get to do. This is what you get to do. Think about what we do for a living. We give life to each other."

After the thought sinks in, I'll add, "Turn to the person next to you and say, 'Do you know what I do for a living? I give life.' Now I want you to literally shout it out." Then I watch as everyone shouts, "I give life. I give life."

A month ago I received the coolest gift. Emma Strain is a patient relations liaison in our Hospital Services Group who visits hospitalized dialysis patients. She often asks them if everything is going okay. "What can I do to help you? Are you feeling okay with your scheduling? Anything I can do for you?"

She sent me an email about something that happened to her at Houston Hobby Airport on her way home after three days at a meeting where I talked to 200-plus teammates about the DaVita Way. Emma wrote that she was in a crowded food court and a gentleman asked if he could sit at an empty chair at her table. They started to chat, and he asked her what she did for a living. Reflecting on what we had talked about earlier that day, she said to him, "I give life."

"Oh, really," he said. "Please do tell."

Emma explained to him what she did in New Orleans, where she worked, and told him about DaVita. "He was a physician from Oklahoma, and we chatted for a while. At the end of the conversation, he said, 'The doctors, the patients, and the families must think you are angels. That is just great patient care.'"

She fought back her tears and thanked him for his kind remark. Emma wrote in her email to me, "I had a big smile on my face and a true sense of fulfillment resonating in my soul. This is the DaVita Way. I *am* the DaVita Way. Thank you for that, Yoda."

I can't imagine a better gift than what I got from Emma.

You probably gathered that DaVita has an unusual company culture. Your first clue probably was that everyone calls me Yoda, and my title is chief wisdom officer. I also told you that the company is referred to as a village and our CEO is known as the village mayor. There is so much more that's uniquely DaVita. For instance, although caring for dialysis patients is a very serious business, having fun is one of our core values. When we get together for meetings, big and small, we do skits to let everyone know that we take having fun very seriously. Our first skit back in 2000 had a Three Musketeers theme. Kent rented uniforms, and he, Joe Mellov, and I walked out on stage as the three famous swordsmen. Our acting left a lot to be desired, but when we raised our swords and said, "One for All, and All for One," it brought the house down. The fact is, now in 2011, there are a lot of people in our "village" who actually believe in "One for All, and All for One."

In another skit and short movie we did, we used the theme from the movie *City Slickers*. Kent was Mitch Robbins, the character played by Billy Crystal. I was Curly, the character played by Jack Palance. Poor Joe, who has had a lifetime fear of horses, gallantly took one for the team, and the three of us rode horses onto the stage. In another skit I was Mickey Mouse, and Joe was dressed as Minnie Mouse. The audience howled, and Joe was such a good sport. I don't think many senior executives in corporate America are willing to dress up, look so ridiculous, and volunteer to have people laugh at them. We did it to make a point . . . and we did. We were willing to act silly and frivolous so we could amuse our teammates and have a good time. Our people understood why we did it, and they appreciated that we were good sports. It's something that many teammates will always remember. Yes, we are in a very serious business. On the clinical side, nearly 140,000 patients with end-stage renal disease literally put their lives in our hands every day. And on the business side, our shareholders expect us to run a profitable organization. But the message I would give the reader is to take what you do seriously, but don't take yourself too seriously. Life is short. I am reminded of a saying from Confucius, "Happy is the man whose work is his play, because he will never have to work a day in his life."

Selling our company culture to 40,000 people is not an easy sale. At first, it seemed hokey, and yes, many people resisted it. But we believed in it, and we didn't let up. When some people started to gradually accept it, the doubting Thomases ridiculed them and said that they drank too much of the Kool-Aid®. We didn't let the initial resistance throw us off track.

In the beginning, we communicated with our teammates openly and honestly about the problems the company was having, and in town hall meetings we told them what we were going to do to fix those problems. And we involved them in the fixes! We gave them dates by which we'd have them fixed. We have a saying at DaVita: "We said, we did!" We delivered what we promised, and in time we earned their trust. Eventually we won them over because we walked the talk. They believed in us—and we believed in them.

Then, when I started telling them to love each other and treat each other the best they possibly can, they accepted this philosophy. The greatest compliment I can receive from a teammate after I give a presentation is "I believe you." I think they believe me because they know that this is truly how I feel about them. I've worked with people who care for kidney patients almost all of my adult life. And I believe they are some of the finest people who walk the planet. I actually do love them. They know Kent and our senior people feel the same way. It's no act. It's genuine. This is something you can't fake. If you do, they'll know it and it will backfire on you. So I warn you—don't even think about saying it unless you absolutely mean it!

I believe that people who come into the health-care field are people who want to live a life like we do. Those who don't feel this way are not going to stay with DaVita. It is not hard to convince the ones who do stay that what they do for a living is "give life." I've heard it said that the number-one need of an employee is to feel good about what he or she does for a living. At DaVita, we do our best to have our teammates go home after work and know what they did that day is GIVE LIFE!

★ Barry's and Bob's Comments ★

Doug Vlchek has a passion for his work, and he's on a mission to make the world a better place. Vlchek strongly believes in what he does. This comes through loud and clear to the people he works with. Conviction is a strong persuader, and we believe it's essential to be a top salesperson. What Vlchek sells is an intangible product. He sells it to large audiences, and he sells it to individuals on a one-on-one basis. His conviction cannot be denied. We are sure you've heard many times that you must be sold on the product and the service you provide before you can effectively sell it to others. Vlchek has built a successful career based on his beliefs. And those beliefs start by his believing in himself.

DaVita is a $6 billion company, and to a large measure, its success has been built by its top management's ability to convince its people to believe in themselves and that their jobs are to give life—to serve each other. This translates into serving their patients. Such a lofty goal can be achieved when it comes from the heart. And if it doesn't, it's a sham that would certainly be uncovered and backfire. As individuals, we can emulate what DaVita does day in and day out. We strongly recommend it. Those who follow this advice will most likely be amply rewarded with a successful career.

20

A Magical Moment

Joe Bourdow

Former President, Valpak Direct Marketing Services Inc.

★ ★ ★

Joe Bourdow served as president of Valpak, the nation's largest local cooperative direct-mail advertising company, until he retired in late 2009 after a 32-year career there. He remains a part-time senior advisor. Founded in 1968, Valpak prints and mails 20 billion-plus coupons from an estimated 60,000 individual advertisers throughout the United States and Canada. Valpak envelopes reach more than 40 million homes every month. The company has 185 franchise offices and company-owned locations in North America. Valpak is also a leading distributor of advertiser offers on the internet and other digital devices.

Bourdow graduated from the University of Virginia in 1973. He was planning a career as an American history teacher but took a local radio job instead. Five years later he was the station manager of WTON in Staunton, Virginia, a position he held until discovering a Valpak envelope in his mailbox. In 1978 he joined the local Valpak franchisee in Richmond, Virginia, as a sales representative and later became a franchisee himself. Between 1978 and 1991, Bourdow was a successful Valpak multifranchise owner. He and his partners also owned a successful local advertising magazine and WKEU AM-FM radio station in Georgia. In 1991 he went to work for corporate Valpak and was named president of the company in 1996.

In 2010 Bourdow started a new venture, Play-by-Play Sports Properties LLC. He is on the board of directors of the International Franchise Association.

★ ★ ★

A couple of weeks before Christmas in 1989, when I was a Valpak franchisee in Richmond, Virginia, I phoned Jim Caroon, who owned Caroon Firestone in Fredericksburg, about 90 minutes away. Jim had been a customer for about six months.

"Jim, it's Joe Bourdow with Valpak," I said. "I called to thank you for your business and wish you a Merry Christmas."

"Very nice," he said, "and I appreciate your call. But if you really want to thank me, you could get me a bottle of 18-year-old Chivas Regal. Now that would truly be appreciated."

"It sure would," I said. "Happy holidays, Jim."

I had another customer in Richmond who was in the same shopping center where the Firestone store was. I had a great relationship with her, and she had a wonderful sense of humor. I called her and said, "Betty, would you do me a big favor?"

"Sure, Joe, what can I do for you?" she asked.

"There's an ABC liquor store in the shopping center. I need you to pick up a bottle of Chivas Regal, an 18-year-old bottle, and drop it off at Carron Firestone. Please attach a card to it that reads, 'Jim, Merry Christmas and happy new year.' And be sure to sign my name."

"No problem," she said.

"I need you to do it right away."

"What's the rush?"

I told her about my conversation with him and said, "I just hung up the phone with him a few minutes ago. If you can do this right away, it will really surprise him that it was delivered so fast."

"I get it," she laughed. "I'll do it immediately. I'll have it to him in less than 20 minutes." Like I said, Betty had a good sense of humor.

"It's expensive," I told her. "The 18-year-old bottle sells for around 50 bucks. Call me back, and I'll send you a check to reimburse you."

"No sweat," she said. "I know you're good for it, Joe."

"Thanks, Betty. I owe you one."

Betty dropped off the bottle at the store, leaving it on Jim's desk while he was in the bay with some of his guys who were putting tires on cars. When he walked into his office, it was just sitting there with my note.

He called me immediately. "Joe, how in the world did you ever do that?"

"Do what?" I asked.

"Get that bottle on my desk like you did."

"Jim, my job is to take good care of my great customers and good friends. I was just doing my job."

"Joe, I just walked into my office and like magic, there it was. For crying out loud, I just got off the phone with you. How did you get it here so fast?"

"A magician doesn't reveal his secrets," I said. "You know we have a code, don't you?"

He laughed and said, "Joe, you're the best."

⋆ Barry's and Bob's Comments ⋆

This short story teaches a valuable lesson about how going an extra mile for a customer sets a salesperson apart from the competition. Not only did Bourdow demonstrate to his customer that he cared about him, his action showed that he was creative in doing something different that surprised him. The customer never forgot what Bourdow did and has retold the story many times since. Not only did Caroon become a longtime customer, over the years he referred many customers to Bourdow.

A Breakthrough Sale

Stephen Rauch

President and CEO, ADB Airfield Solutions

★ ★ ★

*S*tephen Rauch is the president and CEO of ADB Airfield Solutions, located in Columbus, Ohio, which provides airfield lighting products, systems, solutions, and services to airports worldwide. He joined ADB in 1982 as operations manager and stayed with the company after it was acquired by Siemens in 1987. In 1995, Rauch and his family, including four children, moved to Belgium, where he was appointed manager of global operations with a mission to drive operational improvements through the implementation of continuous improvement and lean manufacturing concepts. To lead a turnaround of the company's U.S. operations, in 1997 Rauch was named CEO of ADB in Columbus.

Through implementation of a new sales and customer-focused strategy, revenue has grown nearly 500 percent and has established ADB as the recognized market leader in customer service and innovation. In 2007 Rauch was named general manager for Siemens Traffic Solutions located in Austin, Texas, in addition to his ADB responsibilities, and in 2009 he was part of a management buyout team that purchased ADB from Siemens.

Rauch enjoys many outdoor sports. He and Robin, his wife of 32 years, are avid cyclists and participate in many fundraising events, including the Pelotonia. Practicing his view that people should not go through life with "catcher's mitts on both hands," Rauch has been active in several missions and humanitarian work in Ukraine after the breakup of the Soviet Union and in Kosovo after the 1990s conflict ended. With four children, Rauch has coached many years of various youth athletics. He has also served as a mentor for students in The Ohio State University MBA program. Rauch has a B.S. in operations management and an MBA from The Ohio State University.

I t's never easy for a small company to take business away from the industry leader. Back in the late 1980s, this was the scenario at my company, which had never closed a deal with a large airport. This is what I was up against as head of operations when I flew down from Columbus, Ohio, to Florida to meet with Henry Pruitt, the electrical contractor who would be installing lighting at the Orlando International Airport. Pruitt's company was a subcontractor for the general contractor who had been awarded the contract by the airport to put in an additional runway. Today our annual revenues are in the $100 million range, but back then we only grossed $6 million a year. Our $1 million bid for the job was in line with the competition so price was not an issue. My job was to convince Pruitt that my small firm could do the work I said we could do.

A courteous man, he politely listened to my presentation. "I never heard of ADB Airfield Solutions," he said. "What airports currently have your lighting?"

"We've been doing airport lighting since the 1950s," I told him. "We're a Belgian firm, and we've lighted a lot of airports on the other side of the pond."

"That's well and good," he said, "but I'm not interested in what your firm has done abroad. What airports have your lighting in the United States?"

"We've done a lot of work for county airports across the country," I answered.

"I don't care about your small airport customers," he said. "As we both know, large airports set the fixtures down in the concrete. Isn't it true that county airports have elevated lights? It's not as if your company would do the same work with a big airport such as ours but on a larger scale. The way I look at it, Steve, other than the fact that small ones and big ones are both airports, the similarity ends there."

"You're right, Henry," I agreed. "Even though we haven't done a large airport project in the USA, we have excellent products and that are FAA approved. ADB has vast experience in airport lighting, and we believe we can do the big airports in the U.S. market."

"My concern is that your company is an unknown quantity," Pruitt said. "You simply don't have the résumé. It's not only my company that you'll be dealing with, Steve. My customer is the general contractor, and it's much easier for me to tell him that I gave the job to a known quantity rather than ADB, a tiny firm neither he nor I have ever done business with. In fact, I'd wager he's never heard of ADB. I know I hadn't before you called to make an appointment to see me. What's more, you can't even give me a reference from a large airport that can vouch for the good work you do. Like mine, the general contractor's reputation is on the line with the end user, the Orlando airport. If something goes wrong with the lighting, we look like fools for having chosen a small, unknown company. On the other hand, if we go with a big company that's a known quantity in the airport business and it does a poor job, it's a matter of 'who would have ever known?' If your company screws up, the blame is put on us for choosing you. Do you see where I'm coming from, Steve? I'm held accountable by the general contractor and the end user, the airport."

"I do, Henry, and I appreciate your being candid with me," I answered.

"This project is 15 times bigger than anything your company has ever done," he said. "Doing the lighting for a big airport like ours is much different from those little airports you've worked with."

"True, but it doesn't mean we can't do a big one." I paused and added, "You know, Henry, there was a time when my competitor never did a big job."

I had done my homework before I went to Orlando, and I knew that the company I was competing against did 80 percent of the airport lighting business in the U.S. I also had been told that they had become arrogant. Their success had gone to their heads, and they were in a fat, dumb, and happy mode. They had a take-it-or-leave-it attitude, and the word was out throughout the industry that they were unpleasant to do business with. From a few things Pruitt said, I surmised he didn't particularly like them. But they were a known quantity in the industry. We were not. It was a catch-22, the old story, "Well, you don't have the experience." But how do you get the experience or prove yourself if you don't get a contract with a big airport? I knew if we got this job and did it right, it would put us on the map. It would be our ticket to doing jobs for other big airports.

I also understood that a good salesperson knows what drives a customer to make a buying decision. There are several drivers in our field. Of course, price is a driver, but our numbers and theirs were in the same ballpark. A second driver is the execution of a project. A third driver is follow-up. At the end of the day, you've got to do what you say you will do. If you don't, nothing else matters. The competing company had a reputation of failing to make deadlines, and when that happens, it could slow up the general contractor's entire schedule.

This project had three customers to please, each with different drivers. The end user has a different view on things than does the electrical contractor. The airport was more interested in life-cycle costs and how we can help them in the long run. The electrical contractor is looking at the project schedule and how that's going to work. He wants to make sure we have the capability to follow the schedule. The general contractor wants to make sure the subcontractors are reliable and don't slow down the entire project by failing to do their work on time. The actual lighting products were all governed by FAA specifications, so they were a nonissue. Knowing what the drivers were, I focused on letting Pruitt know how much we wanted the business and kept assuring him that we would not disappoint him.

Although I had never done a big airport project, I knew the airport lighting business, and the more we talked the more clear it became in my mind that I knew enough about the project and the execution phase to do an excellent job.

"We will do whatever it takes," I assured him. "If we have to work around the clock to ship things in time to meet your schedule, that's what we will do." I let that thought sink in and added, "Is the competitor going to do that?" I knew that they had a reputation for failing to make deadlines, so this was food for thought for Pruitt. I also knew that they were unionized, and our small, flexible work team wouldn't be restricted by rules that might slow down the project execution.

Knowing that putting in an airport runway is a process that takes a year or so to complete, I assured him that I would personally be involved. "I will be the one who monitors the schedule, and I will make trips down here to make sure everything goes smoothly," I vowed. "I will ask questions such as, 'Are we on track?' 'Where are we making mistakes?' 'How's it going?' and so on."

I could see he liked what I was telling him. "We have a reputation with our customers," I added, "that when there is a problem, we are not going to walk away from it. We are going to fight until it's resolved. And it doesn't matter if it's our problem or some other problem, we will get to the bottom of it and take care of it."

At the same time, I was careful not to oversell. I didn't want to make any promises that I couldn't deliver on because I knew that would come back to haunt me. If he asked a question that I couldn't answer, I simply said, "I don't know, but I will find out and get back to you." Like I said, the competitor was arrogant and hard to work with.

I grew up in the country and am basically a humble person. My father always told me, "Little dogs pee on big wheels, son," which always reminds me who I am and that I should never try to pass myself off as a big shot. I think the contrast between my arrogant competitor and our company was so extreme that it gave Pruitt something to think about. He had a choice: "Which of these two companies do you really want to do business with?" In the end, he preferred to do business with my company.

"You are not going to regret making this decision," I assured him, "because we are going to prove to you that we are far and away the best supplier for you out there. And when the job is completed, I don't want you to compare us only to our direct competition. I want you to compare our service to what you get from your very best supplier. When it comes to service, we will raise the bar."

Shaking my hand, he said, "I believe you will."

★ Barry's and Bob's Comments ★

This was a breakthrough sale for Rauch's company, a turning point that opened the door for ADB to go from being a small-time player to the industry's leader. The moral to this story is that unless you think like a big leaguer, you'll never get out of the minor leagues. If you want to land big accounts, go after them. It has an excellent lesson for startup company owners and entrepreneurs. Remember, big companies weren't always big; they started out as small companies. Coca-Cola was founded by John Pemberton, an Atlanta pharmacist who concocted a fragrant caramel-colored syrup meant to be a remedy to cure common ailments.

When he added cold water and soda to it, customers bought it as a refreshing beverage. American Express started out delivering mail as the Pony Express. And Michael Dell started Dell Computers in his college dorm room. These examples serve as reminders that you can start small while dreaming big.

Rauch earned this important sale by being well-prepared, knowledgeable, and, above all else, humble. The competitor that had dominated the field lost out because its people became caught up in their self-importance and were condescending to customers. Rauch says that that competition's 80 percent market share has since fallen to 20 percent. "And what's so profound is that they are still arrogant," he adds. "It's ingrained in their corporate culture." Today, ADB does an estimated 65 to 70 percent of the airport lighting in the United States.

Rauch is cognizant of his competitor's downfall, which serves as a constant reminder of how too much success can be a destructive force. "We are now the industry leader, and in this role we operate with a paranoia model," he points out. "We work hard to get customers, and we work hard to keep them. All the while, we are constantly worrying about who's out there trying to take our customers away. This keeps us on our toes and from becoming complacent. We are always looking for ways to keep improving what we do."

Selling the Dream

Vincent L. Morvillo, Jr.

Owner, Sea Lake Yacht Sales

★ ★ ★

Vince Morvillo is the owner of Sea Lake Yacht Sales in Kemah, Texas, located on Galveston Bay, just 20 minutes south of Houston. Prior to starting his company in 1985, he was an executive vice president for Houston Ventures Inc., a venture capital company with portfolio investments in the medical, manufacturing, organic foods, and precious metals reclamation industries.

Morvillo was severely vision-impaired at birth, progressing to blindness by age 20. But being blind never seemed to handicap him. He graduated with a B.A. at California State University in San Jose in 1968 and earned an MBA at the University of Houston *in 1984. In 2004, he won the Ensign National Championship at Newport, Rhode Island, the only blind person in history to win a national yachting championship. He received Houston's Good Skipper Award for community service, mainly for his fundraising role for Boys and Girls Harbor. He was also named an Honorary Admiral in the Texas Navy for outstanding achievement and community service.*

He is a past president of the Yacht Brokers Association of America and currently serves on the YBAA board of directors. Morvillo is also a sought-after motivational speaker.

★ ★ ★

Knowing all about your product and being an expert in your field is great. I'm all for it. Isn't everybody? But equally important is knowing all about your customer. I've seen many salespeople who know everything there is to know about selling yachts, and they've worked hard to come up with a good sales presentation, so what do they do? Determined to tell everything they know about their product, they tell it all to every prospect, whether he wants to hear it or not!

A good salesperson doesn't overwhelm people with unnecessary information. For example, it isn't necessary to tell the complete history of the company to everyone, nor does every person want to know the exact details about how the product is manufactured. If a guy has one pain, you give him one aspirin. If he's got three pains, you give him three aspirins and that's it. You don't have to give him the whole bottle. If you do, he'll overdose, and you'll kill him. You can kill a sale the same way. This is why I ask a lot of questions of everybody who comes in to buy a yacht. By doing this, I am able to zero in on his needs. In particular, I want to find out what his dreams are, and I find out by listening carefully to what he says. If a shotgun approach is taken, it becomes a hit-or-miss kind of thing.

Let me tell you about how I did this when Mike Hamilton and his wife, Sarah, came in to buy a boat. A couple in their early 60s, they had their 7-year-old granddaughter Avery with them. I introduced myself and said, "Are you from the Galveston area?"

"No, we live near Lake Travis, a 60-mile-long lake near Austin."

"Good for you," I said. "I've been there. It's beautiful down there."

"Like heaven," he said. "It's a big lake so we're looking for a big sailboat."

"What do you envision yourself doing when you own one?" I asked.

"Sailing has always been an important part of my life," he answered. "We have eight grandkids, and I'd like to spend time with them sailing on the lake."

"Eight grandchildren," I said. "That's wonderful."

"I want to spend some one-on-one time with them," Mike continued. "They watch way too much TV. I want to get them away from the TV and their video games. Besides, I'm semiretired and will soon retire, so I can see the two of us spending a lot of time on the boat, just relaxing and enjoying ourselves."

"Do you envision spending the night on the boat?"

"We do," Sarah said, her face lighting up, "so we'll need something with sleeping accommodations."

"Tell me a little about what you picture you'll do with this boat," I said.

"Some days we might go out, find a nice cove where we'll dock and just splash around in the water," she said.

"Or just get away on a lazy day and read a book," he said.

"Do you have a certain price in mind?" I asked him.

"Somewhere below $200,000," he said.

"Do you have something in particular in mind?" I asked.

"I don't have a particular brand in mind," he said. "I'd like it to be a fairly big boat, 42 feet or so. But most important, I want to take my grandkids on it. Most of the time, I can see just one or maybe two of them with me. They're little, so I'll have to single-hand the boat. If it's too big, it will take two people, so that won't work."

"With what you tell me, Mike," I said, "the right size boat for you is a 40-footer."

"I was thinking about something a little bigger," he said.

"I have several 42- and 44-foot boats I can show you, but you can't single-hand them. That will mean you can't spend that one-on-one time with one of your grandkids. Another thing, the bigger ones will be more than 200 grand."

"Let's have him show us some 40-foot boats," Sarah said, "and we can see if they seem big enough."

I showed them four 38-foot boats. Sarah liked the sleeping accommodations in one of them. Its price was $175,000, well within their budget.

"It's not quite as big as I wanted," he said.

"I could sell you a bigger boat, and it will cost you more money that will go over your budget," I said. "You do know that with a bigger boat, you won't be able to spend that quality one-on-one time with your grandkids."

"I know, but I had something slightly bigger in mind," he said.

"Tell me about what you think the criteria would be for the perfect boat for you," I said.

"Like I said, it would be 42 feet, maybe even 44 feet, have good sleeping accommodations, and be in the $200,000 price range."

The 38-foot boat selling for $175,000 met all of his criteria, with the exception that it was somewhat smaller than what he said he was looking for.

"Mike, I think the 38-foot boat meets nine out of ten of your criteria," I said. "Now is it perfect for you? No, but you will never find perfection. It doesn't exist. If we go above 40 feet, it will exceed your budget, and you won't be able to go enjoy that one-on-one time with your grandkids."

"He's right," his wife said. "Isn't that your objective, honey?" Then turning to me, she said, "He's told me that so often, I hear it in my sleep. I think the 38-foot boat is exactly what we should buy."

He wasn't sure what to do, and I could see that he was frustrated because he couldn't make a decision. "Mike, can you envision yourself out on your boat with one of your grandkids?" I paused and waited for his response.

"Yes," he said.

"Now what do you envision if you don't move forward on this boat? What's going to happen?"

"I don't know," he said. "Someone else is going to buy it?"

"That could happen. What else?"

"You know what?" he answered. "I won't have that one-on-one time I want to enjoy with my grandkids."

"Mike, this is your dream," I assured him. "You deserve it."

"You are right," his wife said, "and as you always say, Mike, 'You only live once.'"

"She's right," I said.

"I know it," he said.

Throughout the sale, their granddaughter Avery was sitting on his lap like an angel. But about an hour had expired from the time they came in, and she was starting to get a little antsy.

"Avery, come over here," I said.

She got off his lap and came to me, and I whispered in her ear. With that, she said, "Popa, let's buy the boat."

They both laughed, and he said to her, "Okay, Avery, if this is what you want, we will."

"Good work, Avery," I laughed. "I owe you part of my commission."

At this point, my blindness served as an advantage. I said to him, "Okay, now this is the part where you get to write the contract because I can't do that."

They laughed and I continued. "Since you are going to write the contract, you get to sit in this chair, and I am going to the other side of the desk."

I stood up and motioned to him to change seats with me and we did. When we were both seated, I said, "Now I want you to fill out the blanks." I had memorized the contract, and I instructed him on how to complete it, which he did.

Without asking him for his approval, I said, "Okay, Mike, there's a place at the bottom for you to put your signature." And that's what he did. "Now, do you see that place at the bottom that asks for the deposit check number? Take out your checkbook."

He did, and I said, "What's the next check number?" He told me, and I said, "Good. Write it in there." I didn't have to ask him to write out the check because that's what he automatically did.

We had the boat transported to where he wanted it delivered, and about a month later, I gave him a call. "Mike, how's it going? Are you enjoying your boat with the grandkids?"

"I had them out last weekend," he said. "We had such a good time. You know what? My little grandson is learning to steer the boat. Vince, you were so right. I can't thank you enough for putting me into this boat. I keep thinking about what it would be like had I bought a bigger boat. We wouldn't be able to have the kind of fun we're having now. How can I thank you?"

"You just did," I answered.

⋆ Barry's and Bob's Comments ⋆

As Vince Morvillo says so appropriately, "People buy dreams." There is only one way to find out what their dreams are. Ask them, and listen carefully to what they tell you. Morvillo asks people about what they envision doing once they actually own a yacht. What he hears runs the gamut.

"A person may tell me, 'I'm looking for a way to get away from my busy job. I need time to relax.' I'll then ask, 'How do you see yourself relaxing on this boat? Could you tell me what relaxing things you would be doing?' Someone else tells me, 'I just want to get away with my friends and forget about work. Just laugh and have a good time.' Everyone has a different definition of how to relax, so I let them tell me about it." Morvillo emphasizes that you can't sell someone until you find out what he wants. "I talk about their dreams because it's about them. You must always remember what selling is about. It's all about the customer."

We concur that salespeople in many fields sell dreams. People buy investments, homes, automobiles, life insurance policies, and many other products and services to fulfill their dreams. No matter what you sell, how often have you heard a prospect say, "I've dreamed about this all my life"? If you listen, people will tell you about their dreams. You'll hear them talk about their dream house, their dream vacation, how they dream about their children going to a good college, and how they dream about what they'll do when they retire. Real estate agents, life insurance agents, and financial advisors sell products and services that fulfill those dreams.

Another thing happens when people express their dreams. By saying them out loud, they verbally paint a visual picture in their minds about what it is like to own your product or service. This reinforces their desire and justifies their buying decision. Unfortunately, most salespeople are so anxious to make a sale, they talk too much, overselling when they should shut up and listen. Truly good professional salespeople let their customers talk. By doing so, they sell themselves.

Knowing Your Customer's Passion

Catherine L. Hughes

Founder, Chairperson of the Board, Radio One Inc.

★ ★ ★

Catherine Hughes is the founder of Radio One Inc., one of the nation's largest radio broadcasting corporations and the largest radio broadcasting company that primarily targets African-American and urban listeners. Radio One has a daily audience of 18 million listeners. Based in Washington, DC, Radio One owns and operates 52 radio stations located in 16 urban markets in the United States (Atlanta, Baltimore, Boston, Charlotte, Cincinnati, Cleveland, Columbus, Dallas, Detroit, Houston, Indianapolis, Philadelphia, Raleigh-Durham, Richmond, St. Louis, and Washington, DC). Hughes' media enterprises also include Interactive One LLC, majority interest in TV One LLC, *a cable/satellite network targeted to an African-American audience, and Reach Media Inc., home of the Tom Joyner Show.*

When Radio One was listed on the NASDAQ stock exchange in 1999, Hughes became the first African-American female to head a publicly traded corporation. As of 1997, her son, Alfred Liggins III, has been CEO and president of Radio One.

Hughes attended Creighton University and moved to Washington, DC, in 1971 when she became a lecturer in the newly established School of Communications at Howard University. She entered radio in 1973 as general sales manager at WHUR, Howard University Radio. During her first year, the station's revenue went from $250,000 to $3 million. In 1975, Hughes became the first female vice president and general manager of a station in the nation's capital and created the format known as the Quiet Storm, the most listened-to urban radio format in the United States, airing on more than 450 stations. In 1980, Hughes purchased her first station, WOL-AM, in Washington, DC.

In 2000, Radio One was named "Company of the Year" by Black Enterprise. Fortune *ranked it one of the "100 Best Companies to Work For."* Essence *named Hughes one of the "100 Who Have Changed the World," and both* Regardie's *and* Washingtonian *magazines named her one of the "100 Most Powerful and Influential Persons."* Ebony *named her one of the "10 Most Powerful Women in Black America."*

★ ★ ★

P rior to acquiring Radio One in 1980, I was vice president and general manager of Howard University's radio station, WHUR, based in Washington, DC. At the time, McDonald's created an urban advertising budget, and to get advertising dollars for WHUR through McDonald's ethnic budget, I called on Tony Washington. Tony was an African-American executive with Needham, Harper & Steers, which at the time was the city's biggest ad agency. I made an appointment to pitch him on buying time, and although he was very cordial, I couldn't convince him to buy from our station.

"What could be more ethnic than Howard University-owned WHUR?" I asked him.

"It's your billing system," Tony said. "I know all about it. The university has not set it up as a separate entity."

"We can work around that," I answered.

"I've heard horror stories about it and how advertising agencies literally get billed for tuition and books. The billing mistakes are legendary. The billing snafus and the errors that you all are making border on being hilarious. But it's no laughing matter. I don't want to risk messing up this account for the future of urban radio because you all don't have your billing set up correctly."

"I could fix it," I assured him.

"I'm sorry, Cathy," he said politely, and that was the end of the conversation.

I wasn't about to go away without getting some advertising dollars from Tony. Because he was so friendly, every time I called requesting a meeting, I'd get in to see him. He'd ask me about the station and always had words of encouragement, but still no sale. It was frustrating because Tony was so respectful and genuinely interested in WHUR. I've made thousands of calls on prospects, and when most of them don't buy, they don't generally give you a reason. They say something vague like, "We don't think it's timely," or, "We are committed for the rest of the year." Tony was straightforward, but just the same, the end result was no sale!

"I don't get it," I once said to him. "It's the McDonald's urban budget. McDonald's created a budget exclusively for companies that cater to black consumers. WHUR totally caters to an African-American audience."

"WHUR is a college student station," he answered. "Sorry, Cathy."

I had run into this objection before, and I knew that there were advertisers who didn't view us as a viable commercial outlet because we were owned by a college. It was the number-one objection I'd get from big advertisers. They did not place time on college stations.

"But McDonald's wants to reach the black consumer," I told Tony.

"Good point," he'd say, but still no sale. I felt as though I was up against a brick wall, but I wasn't going to quit. As long as the door was open, I was determined to keep calling on him. And the door was always open. Tony would always find time to talk to me.

On one of my calls I bumped into his mother in the lobby, waiting to have lunch with Tony. She and I started to talk, and we formed a friendship. We would meet for lunch, and I even tried to get her to intervene. She tried to help me, but still he kept turning me down. Most important, his mother was a great source of information about her son. Through her, I was able to learn a lot about Tony. For instance, I learned that he was one of 11 children. He was the one who always helped his mother. She told me about how in his college days, Tony was always organizing various relief efforts for communities in trouble. "My son has always been committed to improving his community," she said.

Once I knew what his hot buttons were, I stopped selling him on advertising with Howard University. I switched gears and focused on convincing him to help the university straighten out its media outlet. "With the powerful signal that Howard University has in the market," I told Tony, "we have a tremendous opportunity to do something that's never been done before in urban radio." His eyes glistened. This got his attention. By knowing what his mother told me and from what I observed by having many conversations with Tony, I appealed to his need to give back to the African-American community.

"Radio is a cultural experience in the African-American community," I said. "This is why commercials work better when they are aired on a black outlet. There is a credibility factor that black-owned media brings to the table that goes back to the days of Frederick Douglass, a revered historical figure. Douglass was in the newspaper business. It was his abolitionist paper, *The North Star*, that helped to establish his credibility."

"I couldn't agree more," he said.

"Black media has always been the source of pertinent information in our community," I continued. "What we're doing at WHUR is much more than a regular entertainment outlet. This is far more than pure radio entertainment. This is the dissemination of pertinent information that will help our listeners upgrade their lives and their lifestyle."

'You make a good point," he confirmed.

"Black radio is different than any other medium in the communications industry," I stressed. "Second only to the black church is the relationship between the black consumer and black radio. Mainstream media is busy serving their audience. And black participation has always been viewed as an onlooker or a second thought."

Tony kept nodding his head in agreement. I knew I was getting to him. If I had learned anything from Tony Washington, it was that he is the ultimate salesperson who thinks that when you say "No" to him, it means you haven't made up your mind yet. My problem is that when you tell me "No," I accept it at face value. It sometimes hurts my feelings. It sometimes angers me. But not Tony. He keeps selling until he makes the sale.

After many conversations with him, I said, "I'm a creative person, Tony. My mother was a professional musician. She had a world-renowned orchestra, an 18-piece all-girl band called the International Sweethearts of Rhythm. I get my creativity from her. I created 'The Quiet Storm,' which is the number-one format in the history of urban radio. My strong suit is programming. I know a lot more about programming than I do about selling. I can create good programming, but I am not the best representative to sell my product. You are someone who I know can sell ice to an Eskimo. I want you to come with us at WHUR and together, we can make a difference. We can do something important for our community."

At the time, Tony had a six-figure job at Needham, Harper & Steers, and there was no way WHUR could come anywhere near matching what they were paying him. Tony was considered *the* master salesman in the entire marketplace. However, I was able to convince him to leave his agency job and help me establish the radio station. The station never got any business from McDonald's ethnic budget while Tony was with the agency, but after he came to work at WHUR, he went back and pitched them. We did get some business for the station.

After I left WHUR and bought WOL, Tony took a job with a TV station. Two years later, he came back and became WOL's sales manager. We have worked together ever since, nearly 35 years.

★ Barry's and Bob's Comments ★

Cathy Hughes says that selling Tony Washington on leaving his high-profile, high-paying job to join WHUR was the biggest sale she ever made. "I sold him on the future of black ownership of media," she tells, "and how he could contribute to the black community by building Howard University's station. Once I truly knew the person he was, I knew what it would take to convince him to join forces with me as my sales manager. I strongly believe that good selling is having a clear understanding about the person who is sitting across from you. You must remember that person has many people coming to them to sell something. You are not the only person calling on that individual. This is particularly true when you call on big corporations. All too often, salespeople make sales calls that are too impersonal. They fail to realize that great salesmanship is about building great relationships. Take the time to know your customer. 'Sometimes you become so involved in trying to close the deal,' I tell my sales force, 'that you neglect to know who it is you are selling to. Never forget that when your relationship is on a personal level, the business will eventually come.'"

We concur with Cathy Hughes. Always remember that there is competition out there that also has a good product. The customer has choices, which is why the personal relationship is an important factor in making the sale. We also agree that by taking the time to truly know who it is you are selling, you will learn what his or her passions are. When pointed out, this is so obvious, but most salespeople tend to over-talk and subsequently under-listen. As a consequence, they fail to build personal relationships with their customers and are unable to appeal to their passions.

Little Things Make a Big Difference

Jack Mitchell

CEO, The Mitchell Family of Stores

★ ★ ★

Jack Mitchell is the chairman and CEO of The Mitchell Family of Stores, a three-generation family business that is one of the most successful high-end retail clothiers in the United States, with locations in Connecticut, New York, and California. They are nationally renowned for their personal service touches and strong relationships. Jack and his brother, Bill, were given the business by their parents, who in 1958 had opened a small men's and boy's retail shop in an 800-square-foot storefront in Westport, Connecticut, with a coffee pot and a dream. Bill joined the company in 1965 after graduating from college. Jack, who graduated Wesleyan University in 1962, went on to earn a master's degree in Chinese history at University of California at Berkeley. He then worked as an administrator at a medical and scientific research institute before entering the family business in 1969. Bill's and Jack's seven sons (neither has a daughter) are all active in the business and today own all of the company's shares. Jack's wife, Linda, joined the company in 2000 as vice president of women's merchandising.

Under Bill's and Jack's leadership, The Mitchell Family of Stores has become well known for employee engagement and longevity and providing exceptional customer service and high-quality merchandise in an exciting, friendly, and visually dynamic atmosphere. Legendary for their exceptional customer service, a case study on the company was featured in the Harvard Business School Review *in September 2007.*

In 2003, Jack launched a second career as a speaker and author. His first book, Hug Your Customers: The Proven Way to Personalize Sales and Achieve Astounding Results, *was a* Wall Street Journal *bestseller. In 2008, Jack published his second book,* Hug Your People: The Proven Way to Hire, Inspire, and Recognize Your Employees to Achieve Remarkable Results. *He has become known as a passionate and enthusiastic public speaker, keynoting at more than 200 events.*

Jack and his family have received many community leadership awards from the Anti-Defamation League, The Menswear Division of UJA-Federation of New York, and Sacred Heart University. Jack is on the Yale Cancer Advisory Board and Greenwich Hospital board of trustees.

S everal years ago my brother Bill and I co-chaired a black-tie fund-raising event for the Inner-City Foundation for Charities at the Greenwich Hyatt. With our spouses, we greeted arriving guests. Lou Gerstner , who was the CEO and chairman of IBM, walked in with his wife, Robin. I gave them a warm welcome and immediately, in a very friendly way, she pulled me aside.

"Jack, I have to tell you about the most fabulous thing that happened to me at Richards today."

I knew they were customers at Richards, our store in Greenwich, where they live. And since I always love hearing about customer experiences in our stores, I eagerly said, "Okay, Robin, tell me what was so fabulous at Richards today."

Robin prefaced her story by telling me that she and Lou go to a lot of black-tie affairs. "Last night, we were at an event at the Waldorf, and when Lou got out of the car to button his jacket, a button fell off. He picked the button up and put it in his pocket. But I could see that he felt uncomfortable because all night he was squirming away."

"That's not good," I said.

"As you know, we're longtime Richards customers, but last night Lou wasn't wearing a Richards tuxedo," she said. "I didn't know that when I took it to the store this morning to have the button sewed back on. One of your tailors, Tulio, not only sewed on the button, but do you know what else he did?"

By this time, there were 25 to 30 guests listening to her story, and before I could say anything, Robin continued, "Tulio pressed the pants and the jacket so Lou could look elegant tonight. When I handed him my credit card, he said, 'No, no, Mrs. Gerstner, there is no charge.' No matter how much I tried to persuade him to let me pay, he wouldn't let me."

Of course I was beaming, and I didn't mind it at all that there was a crowd of people who had gathered to hear Robin's high praise for the service she received. Tulio did what we typically do for all our customers when they have a minor problem with suits, sports jackets, and pants. It doesn't matter whether they purchased the merchandise at our store or elsewhere. It could be a hem on a woman's dress, a cuff that needs to be sewed, a loose or lost button—our philosophy is to treat our customers like they are members of our family, and isn't that how people treat family? I know that in our family, we do. If something isn't right, we'll make it right. But I didn't mention this to Robin. I just thanked her for visiting our store and told her how happy I was that we were able to do this for her.

About a year later, a customer invited me to join him in his box at the U.S. Open tennis finals. We were seated next to the IBM box. When Lou spotted me, he came over and gave me a huge high five, which floored me. That wasn't his style, so I surmised he was happy to see me. Then he started telling everyone that Richards/Mitchells are the greatest clothing stores in the world because we sewed on his button and didn't charge him. "Their tailor even pressed my tux for free. Now how is that for great service?"

And how good is that for promoting our business? The CEO of one of the world's largest and most prestigious companies is raving about how much we care about our customers—over a button! What's more, IBM is known in the business world for its exceptional service. Wow! There is nothing better than word-of-mouth praise from a satisfied customer, and when it's Lou Gerstner who's saying all those good things, it is absolutely awesome.

"I got another button story," Lou said a few years later. "Last winter I am on a flight to Asia and the flight attendant takes my topcoat to hang it, and as she did, a button pops off. I didn't think anything about it. However, when we landed in Tokyo and I go to put my coat back on, I was surprised and thrilled to discover that the button had been sewed back on. The next day, in a speech in front of 3,000 people, I spoke about extraordinary customer service and talked about how a little thing like a button can make a big difference in building relationships."

"Great story," I said.

"I now have two button stories to tell when I speak about taking care of customers," Lou laughed, and we gave each other another high five.

★ Barry's and Bob's Comments ★

Jack Mitchell and his family have built a highly successful business based on giving customers exceptional personalized service. Mitchell emphasizes that it's a matter of giving a lot of little "hugs" to customers that show them how much you care for them. It's not that the Mitchells don't also give a lot of big "hugs" to their customers as well—like the time an associate flew from San Francisco to Los Angeles to deliver a suit to a customer who wanted to look his best at an important business meeting the next morning. Then there are the times when one of the Mitchells goes to the store on a Sunday afternoon and opens it for an out-of-town customer who is in desperate need of a tuxedo shirt for a wedding that evening or needs an alteration on a garment. The Mitchells and their team are known for doing things like that and a lot more. This kind of service is second nature to them—it's in their DNA.

Sometimes it is the little things that matter the most. These are things that we all can do for our customers—most hugs are free or cost just pennies, but boy, are they appreciated! And these services build strong customer loyalty for life.

Resourcefulness

Jeff Herman

President, The Jeff Herman Literary Agency LLC

★ ★ ★

*J*eff Herman founded his literary agency in 1987 when he was in his 20s. The New York firm has since relocated, and today is based in Stockbridge, Massachusetts. The agency has sold hundreds of titles to publishers, and today is recognized as one of the most innovative agencies in the publishing industry.

Prior to launching the agency, Herman worked for a New York public relations firm where he designed and managed national marketing campaigns for Nabisco Brands and AT&T, including the introduction of the first consumer cell phone in the New York City market. Upon graduating from Syracuse University, where he was the captain of the award-winning debate team, Herman was hired as a publicist by Schocken Books (now a Random House imprint). While at Schocken, he promoted the bestseller When Bad Things Happen to Good People.

Herman has authored several books, including the widely acclaimed Jeff Herman's Guide to Book Editors, Publishers and Literary Agents, which has more than 500,000 copies in print. He and his wife, Deborah Levine Herman, collaborated on Write the Perfect Book Proposal: 10 Proposals That Sold & Why!

☆ ☆ ☆

Several years ago I held an auction for uber-investor Ken Fisher. John Wiley & Sons outbid *many* other publishers and paid a mid-six-figure advance for *The Only Three Questions That Count.* The book was a *New York Times* hardcover bestseller for many weeks, with sales around 200,000 copies.

Publishers love high-profile authors like Ken Fisher, especially one who operates a successful company that has a strong marketing arm. He is the founder and CEO of Fisher Investments, a company based in Woodland Hills, California. The firm manages a $100 billion portfolio. A self-made billionaire, Ken is on the *Forbes* list of the 400 richest people in America.

To promote the book, Fisher Investments placed full-page ads in *The New York Times*, and Ken appeared on many business TV programs on CNBC, CNN, and the Bloomberg channels. He also made the book visible on his company website, which receives millions of hits per year. Ken was pleased with the results of *The Only Three Questions That Count* because it accomplished what he wanted. First, Ken had his own philosophy about investments that he wanted to express; the book served as a platform to document and broadcast his thinking. Second, he enjoyed promoting the book, and it put him in front of a national audience. The exposure was good for his business.

With his book's success, I wanted Ken to write another one. John Wiley & Sons had an option to publish his next book, and it, too, wanted another. Of course a literary agent and a book publisher like an author to follow up with another book while his or her previous bestselling book is still on the minds of readers. This gives the next book a better-than-even chance to also become a bestseller. The problem was that Ken didn't want to write another book, or at least not any time soon.

"With the momentum that your current book generated," I told him during a phone conversation, "you will have another bestseller. That's impressive, Ken, having back-to-back bestsellers."

"I am sure it is," he politely replied, "but writing one is a lot of work that requires a lot of time. As you know, Jeff, I did all of the writing of my first draft, which meant getting up early in the morning and working after hours. It was a good experience that I enjoyed, but I don't want to do another one."

"The book was good for business," I pointed out, "because it attracted new customers."

"You're right, Jeff, but if I do another one, it could backfire on me."

"How will that happen?" I asked.

"I've got a company to run, and if I keep writing books, my clients are going to start saying, 'Gee, it looks like you have a lot of time to write books.'"

"I understand," I said. "Ken, why don't we give it some thought before we close the door?"

"That's fine with me, Jeff, we'll talk later," he said, ending the conversation.

Naturally, I enjoyed the agent's fees I received from Ken's first book, and I wanted a repeat performance. My wife, Debbie, works with me, and we often talk shop at the dinner table. That night I told her about my dilemma.

"I can't insist Ken write another book," I explained. "I have to find a way to motivate him. But so far I haven't come up with anything."

Thinking out loud, Debbie said, "What does it take to motivate a billionaire? It's not the money that he can earn from a book."

"No. His time is much more valuable when applied to his own business than it is writing books," I said.

"Ken received a lot of publicity from his book. Does he enjoy doing interviews?"

"Yes, and he's very good at it, but again, it's not a good use of his time. And he's done that. He's now on to other things."

"There must be something that we're overlooking," Debbie said.

"I've been thinking about it all day," I answered, "but so far I haven't come up with anything."

There was a long silence and we continued eating.

Then out of nowhere, Debbie said excitedly, "I've got an idea!"

"Okay, let's hear it," I said, placing my fork on my plate, waiting for her reply.

"What about a book imprint?"

I paused to let the thought sink in. Suddenly a light bulb went off. "Brilliant!" I exclaimed. "Honey, you're a genius."

"So that would excite him?" she asked.

"Yes, I think it would. He has all the resources—an in-house staff that is continually generating research, and even better, it's mostly original research. He could call it, 'Fisher Investment Press' and use his own logo. His own brand! And Wiley would be a perfect publisher. It already has several branded imprints. It does Betty Crocker cookbooks, Frommer travel books, the Dummies books . . ."

"Yes, and Morningstar and J.K. Lasser," Debbie enthusiastically added. "And Wiley bought Bloomberg Press."

"With a Fisher Investment imprint, we could be talking about 20-plus books a year," I said. "Now Ken might like this, yes, this just might excite him."

The following day I called Ken. "Let's forget about doing another book," I said. "I've got something much better for you."

"Okay, I'm listening," he said.

"I recommend a Fisher Investments imprint."

"You'll have to explain to me what that would be," Ken replied.

"You will control Fisher Investments Press. You will have your own publishing company, de facto. You will team up with Wiley Publishing, and you will have all the accoutrements of your own publishing house but won't have to do any of the heavy lifting. Wiley already publishes many dedicated branded imprints, and it is very good at it." I told him how Wiley publishes J.K. Lasser, the Dummies guides, the Betty Crocker books, and so on.

"Go on," he said.

"Wiley does all the production," I continued. "It does all the editing. It does all the distribution. It provides all the muscle. But it will be your brand, and it will be on its letterhead. Your brand will appear on all of the marketing material."

"Could we do that?" he asked.

"Yes," I assured him. "And with your own brand, you'll have almost total editorial control, so you'll have considerably more freedom than you did as an author."

"Really?" he said. "I like that."

"Yes, and you will be the only person in your field who has his own publishing company."

"Can you give me some ballpark figures on how much you think this will cost?"

"There is no investment," I assured him, "with the exception of promoting books, but those dollars will be promoting your company, which is what you do anyway."

"We already have the staff to do this," he responded. "Our people could do many books a year. Now this sounds promising, Jeff. Tell you what. Could you put together a business plan explaining how this works? Nothing elaborate, just do a two-pager. It would be helpful for me to have so I can explain it to our people."

"I'll get started on it immediately," I said.

Later that day I emailed a two-page business plan to Ken, and a few days later we had a long telephone conversation. Ken had reviewed the plan, digested it, and, wanting to know exactly what he was getting into, he asked concise questions. At the end of the conversation he said, "Let's do it."

"Okay," I answered, "but there is just one thing I have to do."

"And that is?"

"I have to go to Wiley or another publisher and get them to agree to do it."

"Right," he said. "Will that be hard?"

"If I do it, it's easy," I replied. "If I don't do it, then I guess that means it's hard. I'll have to get back to you."

I called Ken's editors at John Wiley and scheduled an appointment to present the concept in person. Although I typically do most of my business on the telephone, this warranted a visit to Hoboken, New Jersey, for a face-to-face meeting. After all, this was a complicated deal and something I had never done before. At the meeting I explained the entire concept about making Fisher Investment Press a branded, independent imprint within the Wiley family of brands.

"His first book with us was successful," a senior executive said, "and as you know, we have the option on his next book."

"It's not that Ken doesn't want to do a second book with Wiley," I replied. "He's just not motivated to write another book in general any time soon. But if his next book is part of his own imprint, he's likely to see things in a different light."

"Yes, and he was an ideal author to work with," someone said. "His organization did an excellent marketing job, and Ken was very effective with the media."

"Look at it this way," I explained. "Ken has a staff of investment experts who can write 10, perhaps 20, books a year. These will be mostly reference books and come from the in-house research they are already doing for their clients. These books will cover investments on energy, technology, commodities, and so on. They will be targeted to the serious investor. His people can also find outside experts to write books. As you know, Fisher Investments has the resources to market books. And as part of the imprint, I bet Ken will be willing to generate one or two personally authored trade books a year, which will be intended to make the bestseller lists."

I emphasized the support that Fisher Investments made in the first book with Ken and said, "Wiley will have a strong alliance with Fisher Investments, and instead of just locking in one book that will be profitable for Wiley, we are now going to lock you into an ongoing program."

The meeting ended on a positive note, and we soon nailed down a significant seven-figure deal. Upon signing the contract, Wiley invited us in for a celebratory lunch.

Upon consummating the deal, it was crucial that Ken's staff was in harmony with a publishing venture that promised to generate eight-figure revenues within the first 18 months. It was equally vital that the Wiley and Fisher Investments people get to know each other and figure out how to work together.

Fortunately, Wiley agreed to fly a large team of marketing and editorial staff to meet with Ken and his team in California. I explained to Ken why it was important to make as many relevant people as possible available for this meeting.

"Absolutely," he agreed. "Come on out. I'm sure both sides will have many questions to ask each other."

For the program to be successful, Ken's people needed to be included at the initial stages. I also knew that if they weren't sold on the program, they wouldn't be supportive, and if so, it would fail. When I met with them, I explained how Fisher Investments Press would publish specialty books, most or all of which could be done by their internal people, and one or two bestselling trade books authored by Ken. They liked the idea that they would get bylines and the publishing would be an extension of what they already did. The company had an excellent marketing team, and it knew from the media coverage that Ken's previous book received that having a publishing imprint was a wonderful opportunity. And doing something new and different excited the people involved.

To get mutually acceptable contracts written, I probably spent more time with Fred Haring, Fisher Investments' general counsel, than anyone else. As the attorney, his job was to make sure that nothing would come back to bite the firm. He and I had to spend a lot of time crafting language that accomplished what Wiley required without creating unacceptable risks for the firm. From past experience, I know that lawyers can find ways to squelch a deal, sometimes because they want to show how smart they are and other times because they think that's what they're paid to do. This was not true with Fred. He was savvy and understood that his job was to make things happen, not get in the way. Like Ken and the other Fisher people, I enjoyed doing business with Fred.

We closed the deal, and Ken Fisher proceeded to author several more books that spent many weeks on the *New York Times* and many other bestseller lists. And a few dozen specialized investment books have also been published to date, all of which are part of Fisher Investments Press and represented by my agency.

⋆ Barry's and Bob's Comments ⋆

Billionaires are different from the rest of us. Besides obviously having more money, their time is much more valuable. To convince Fisher to do another book, Herman had to come up with something that would capture his interest. As Herman explained, it wasn't money or writing another bestseller that won the day. Fisher had already done that. He was concerned that writing another book would be a distraction and make customers think he wasn't minding the store. For this reason, Herman needed a creative approach that he could sell to Fisher, and if he couldn't, he would have lost a big book sale. Herman presented a big idea to Fisher, something that was much different than merely writing another book. To make the sale, Herman had to convince Fisher that having his own imprint was a unique approach that nobody in the investment industry had ever previously done. Herman assumed, correctly, that Fisher would find the idea appealing. He liked doing things where he could rise above the crowd.

Herman had to make two more sales to make the deal. He had to sell John Wiley & Sons, and he had to sell the people at Fisher Investments to get their support. We salute Herman for going the extra mile by meeting in person with the Wiley executives in Hoboken and later with the Fisher executives in Woodland Hills. We admire his tenacity, which paid off handsomely.

There are times when you must think outside the box and be innovative. When you dare to do something bold and audacious, you may make big sales that otherwise would have been lost. Don't be afraid to swing for the fences. As they say in baseball parlance, "When you hit a home run, you get to walk around the bases."

26

Even a CEO Has to Sell Himself

Thomas L. Millner

President and CEO, Cabela's Inc.

★ ★ ★

I n April 2009, Tommy Millner was named president, chief executive officer, and a member of the board of directors of Cabela's Inc., the giant outdoors retailer and catalog company. Previously, he had worked for 15 years at Remington Arms Company Inc., a leading manufacturer of firearms and ammunition, and for 10 of those years as Remington's CEO from 1999 until he resigned to join Cabela's. From December 2008 until March 2009, Millner also served as CEO of Freedom Group Inc., a holding company that directly or indirectly owns Remington and related companies. In addition, he served as a director of Stanley Furniture

Company Inc. from 1999 to March 2011 and Lazy Days R.V. Center Inc. from 2005 to 2009.

Headquartered in Sidney, Nebraska, and founded in 1961, Cabela's is the world's largest direct marketer of hunting, fishing, camping, and related outdoor merchandise. At the end of 2011, the company owned and operated 36 stores with plans to open four more in 2012. The average store has 155,000 square feet. More than 130 million Cabela's catalogs are mailed each year. According to Internet Retailer, cabelas.com had a monthly average of 11.7 million visits in 2011, and the company's gross sales were $2.6 billion that year.

Millner and his wife live near Cabela's Sidney headquarters, where they raise prize-winning Briards (French sheepdogs).

☆ ☆ ☆

I was in line at a Wendy's when my cell phone rang. "Hello, Tommy, this is Susan Hart with Spencer Stuart. I head Spencer Stuart's global Retail, Apparel & Luxury Goods Practices."

"Could you hold on a moment? I have to pay for my Frosty." I juggled the phone while I took out some money from my wallet. The pause gave me time to digest the call. "Okay, I'm back and can talk now."

The headhunter got right down to business and asked, "Would you be interested in being considered for the CEO job at Cabela's?"

My first reaction was that one of my old fraternity brothers was playing a practical joke on me and had had his secretary make the call. I knew Cabela's quite well because it was one of Remington Arms' three biggest customers. I thought to myself, "Why would this iconic customer-service company even think about me for my all-time dream-job-come-true?"

I sat in my car and sipped my Frosty while Susan talked. I explained to her that I'd never worked a day in my life in retail. "It wasn't by choice," I said. "But it never happened, not even in high school."

"We know that, but the company has a lot of talented retail executives," she said.

"Yes," I answered, "and they totally smoke me in experience."

"There are people who think you're a good candidate for the job, and I recommend you consider it."

I went through the interviewing process, including meeting with the board of directors. In my view, one of the critical tipping points in my favor was that they observed the deep passion I've had throughout my career for the customer. I suppose they picked this up when I took them back to my first job at age 20 just out of college, when I was a furniture rep calling on retail stores in the Rocky Mountains. "I learned early on," I said, "that if you don't take care of your customers, your customers don't take care of you. I learned that lesson well and have applied it throughout my career." Evidently they liked what I said because I got the job.

Right from the start I realized that not only did I have to sell the board to get the CEO position, I had to convince the 14,000 people who worked at Cabela's that I was the right person for the job. Without their support, I could not be an effective leader. Years ago I read Robert Greenleaf's book *Servant Leadership*, which advocated that an organization shouldn't be a pyramid with its leader at the top. On the contrary, the servant leader flips the pyramid upside down and views his role as being at the bottom of the pyramid. In this respect, he is a servant of the organization, not its boss. When things are not working, a good leader first asks, "What am I doing wrong? How am I failing to enable our people to succeed?"

When I first came aboard, I was replacing Dennis Highby, who was retiring after having worked at Cabela's since 1976. Dennis started there at age 27. He was the company's 40th—and first salaried—employee. He was named CEO when the company became publicly owned in 2004. Dennis had been around for a long time and did an excellent job. He was well liked by everyone and would be a tough act to follow. I also knew that Cabela's had a strong corporate culture that focused on customer service and everyone would be watching to see what changes

I'd make. I needed to calm any fears that I might change the culture because I didn't care about customers.

I had seen a lot of new CEOs come into a business and make the mistake of thinking the culture should adapt to them. This doesn't imply that a new CEO doesn't change anything, and over the last few years many changes have been made here. For instance, we've intensified our financial focus on the business and, in particular, the metrics of return on capital and productivity in the stores. In my view that has nothing to do with the foundational component of our business, which is *everything starts and ends with our customers*. I wanted the employees to know we would always adhere to our core principles. Our principles, our core values, are never situational. They are never altered. Our principles don't change in a tough month, a tough quarter, or, for that matter, in a good or bad year. I stressed that if we ever fail our customers, there is nothing we can do to save this enterprise over time.

Cabela's core principles today are the same as when Dick Cabela founded the company in Chappell, Nebraska, in 1961. Working out of his home, he placed a classified advertisement in the Casper, Wyoming, newspaper to sell fishing flies. His wife, Mary, pitched in and sent out their first mailings—mimeographed sheets listing their products. The quality of their flies and the deal they offered were excellent and orders poured in. In time, they added other outdoor-related merchandise. In 1963, Dick's brother, Jim, joined the company. After operating the company out of Dick's kitchen, they moved into a succession of buildings in Chappell; then, in 1969, they moved the company into an old John Deere building in Sidney, 28 miles northwest. In time, the Cabelas sold a broad line of outdoor merchandise, always emphasizing top quality and excellence in customer service. The guarantee listed on their first catalog became a creed that is followed to this day. All items are backed by our Legendary Guarantee. The Cabelas always had a small retail component to their catalog operation. We now have 39 stores, and we're still growing. Today, our retail revenues exceed our catalog and online sales revenues. The company has gone high-tech, and in 2010 our website had 135 million daily unique visitors.

As you can see, vast changes have been made since Dick Cabela first started selling fishing flies in 1961. The company continually makes changes. This is true of all successful enterprises. At Cabela's, everything has been and continues to be subject to change. People change, locations change, products change, technologies change— everything is subject to change, with one exception. The company's core principles never change. To paraphrase Thomas Jefferson, in matters of principle one should stand like a rock; in other matters swim with the current.

Upon arriving here, I knew my first sales job would be to our employees. I started by meeting with the top 50 people in the company. I had one-hour sessions with each of them. We met in my office, and my door was closed. I had no notes in front of me, and I never wrote down a single thing. I find that if you write stuff down, people become more cautious about what they say.

I started every conversation with the question, "What do you think?" And I followed up with questions such as, "What are we doing wrong?" Then I listened. From those meetings, I was able to discern what the company needed to do. I don't take credit for our new strategy being my strategy. It came from listening to the leaders of the company. During my first 45 days, I visited every single store, every distribution center, and every call center in the entire company. I also talked to our employees in town hall meetings. I let them know who I was and what I stood for. I encouraged them to ask questions, to inquire about my background and how I felt about certain things, and so on.

These were informal meetings conducted in a relaxed atmosphere so everyone would feel at ease. "When I was growing up in Newport News, Virginia, my father worked as a milkman," I told them, "so I come from a very humble background. I've hunted since I was 13 years old. I can't believe I get to do this for a living. I've been extraordinarily fortunate and blessed in my career. Every day I come to work I pinch myself. And I pinched myself when I was at Remington. I feel so lucky to the core."

Everywhere I went, I looked at all our folks and I said, "You can count on one thing: I'll give you all I've got. I'll do it every single day." I never talked about financial matters. I never mentioned anything about profitability. Instead, in graphic presentations placed all over the building, I visually demonstrated what we call "Circles of Excellence." These are three concentric rings and at the very center of the first circle is the customer. "The customer is the center of all we do," I emphasized. "We must cherish and delight our customers every day in every transaction. This is why the customer is at the center of these three concentric rings.

"The second ring is our employees. Without great, engaged employees, it simply is not possible to cherish customers. And in the third ring are our shareholders. While we are in business to provide a return to our shareholders, this starts with taking care of the customer. It all starts with our customer. If we treat our customers right, our shareholders will be taken care of."

I used the word "cherish" because it is a very intimate word. It conveys more than customer satisfaction. Cherish is a word reserved for those who we really hold dear in our lives—our spouses, children, parents, grandparents, as well as very close friends. It is reserved for our loved ones. Cherish is the word in my vocabulary I wanted to convey to our organization, and I use it every day to clearly demonstrate I get it. I understand it is the foundation Cabela's is built on. We have a culture of cherishing and delighting our customers. This is what I talk about every day wherever I go.

As I mentioned, Cabela's is headquartered in Sidney, Nebraska. It has a population of 6,000 and is located in the western part of the state, which is known as the Nebraska Panhandle, a few miles north of the Colorado border. It's a five-hour drive due west from Omaha. Many of its citizens are outdoors people who love hunting and fishing. Most important, they have good small-town values, and those values are deeply engrained in the company culture.

I also have a small-town background. When I was in the furniture industry, I was CEO of Pilliod, a company based in a South Carolina town with a population of 1,000. With 2,000 employees drawn from the surrounding region, we were the town's biggest employer. The same thing was true when I headed Remington, which is based in Madison, North Carolina, a town with 2,200 citizens. There, too, we were the town's largest employer. I feel there is something special about people who live in small towns across America, in communities where everyone knows everyone and people care for their neighbors. And look where Cabela's has its warehouses and call centers—they're in places like Sidney, Kearney, North Platte, Grand Island, and Lincoln.

We take pride in the fact that we're located in these communities. And since I got here, at my insistence, anyone who answers the phone is told to say, "Hello, this is Ron in Grand Island, Nebraska," or "This is Sarah and I am in Lincoln, Nebraska." We think our customers appreciate this small touch vs. talking to a telephone operator who's in a foreign country.

I also let our people know that 95 percent of the time I answer my own phone, and when a customer calls me, I don't hide behind my CEO moniker. I return the call. This sends a message to everyone about how much I value our customers. Recently, a customer in Arizona called and demanded to speak to me. I was at a meeting but when my assistant gave me the message, she reported that Mrs. Jones, a customer who was also a shareholder, said, "Tell Mr. Millner I was in the store today, and I couldn't find American-made clothing in the store."

I called her back that same day, and Mrs. Jones could not believe I actually returned her call. I listened to her complaint, and I answered, "Mrs. Jones, there is nothing that would make me happier than to buy more American products, but we can't find factories anymore in the United States that make clothing. It is very, very difficult." By the end of the conversation, she was very understanding and told me how much she appreciated my call and explanation.

It is probable she will tell her friends I returned her call, and they will tell their friends, so it's just good business to have made that call. But then, why shouldn't I have called her back? I'm not a king. I'm a person who has a great job, and I understand that one interaction with one customer makes a difference.

In time, I earned the respect and support of the 14,000 employees who work at Cabela's. I might add it was something I didn't take for granted because I was the CEO. I had to earn it. I think some new CEOs make the mistake of trying to make a first impression by having the company make a hard right turn and then they start chasing rainbows. I made it very clear to the organization that I accepted the job because I thought we had, and have, a great company. "We're not going to change what we do," I emphasized. "We are not going to chase pots of gold at the end of rainbows. We are going to get back to the fundamentals of what makes our company successful. And that is customer service, customer service, customer service. And we are going to say it over and over again. And when we are tired of talking about it, we are going to say it a hundred million more times."

Someone sent me an obituary of James Allen (Jimmy) Mose of Casa Grande, Arizona, who died at age 54. It appeared in *The Clearwater (Florida) Progress* newspaper on March 3, 2011. I was so touched by it that I carry it in my wallet and have since read it to thousands of our employees. It reads:

> *James served in the U.S. Army and was a truck driver and worked at a Walmart Distribution Center. He enjoyed camping, hunting, fishing, four-wheeling, and shopping at Cabela's.*

When I read this to our people I say, "The cherishing of our customers is reciprocated by their cherishing us, as witnessed by being in someone's obituary. How many retail companies in the world have ever had that happen?"

★ Barry's and Bob's Comments ★

In an interview Tommy Millner comes across as down-to-earth, someone who you automatically like and admire. Unlike many CEOs who are egotistical and self-centered, he is a humble man who believes his mission is to serve others. Not one to sit in an ivory tower, far removed from employees and customers,

Millner spends a large percentage of his time outside his office. He wisely chose this route when he joined Cabela's, realizing that as an outsider who was picked for the CEO position, it was imperative that he sell himself to Cabela's employees. And while we sometimes don't think about how a CEO must sell his people, it is a big sales job—perhaps the most important sales job a new CEO makes.

What better way for Millner to do it than by praising the company culture and by announcing that its sacred principles would never be changed! We salute Millner's approach. Rather than communicating His message through the normal channels, he personally met with senior company managers and visited all stores, warehouses, and call centers. By doing so, Millner let everyone know that keeping the company culture intact was his highest priority.

The Million-Dollar Offer

Stephen Michella

Vice President, Eggland's Best

★ ★ ★

S tephen Michella is vice president–sales of Eggland's Best, a company that produces the number-one branded egg in the U.S. Prevention *magazine named the company's eggs one of* "The Healthiest Foods for Women." To assure freshness, the company delivers eggs within 24 to 48 hours of laying.

Michella has worked at Eggland's Best since 1992. Upon graduating from Fordam University in 1979, he worked for five years as a sales rep and district manager at Carnation Companies. From 1984 to 1992 he worked as a district manager and then as a division manager at Sara Lee. When he joined Eggland's Best, the company was just starting and had no accounts. It has since *enjoyed spectacular growth, and much credit is given to Michella's sales and sales management talent.*

★ ★ ★

I was on my way to meet with an egg buyer who worked for a national grocery store chain, one of the biggest in the world. While we did a lot of business with this retailer, the volume had reached a plateau that I felt was nowhere near its full potential. That morning I was determined to walk out of his office with a bigger order than we generally received.

Having worked closely with this buyer over the past few years, there wasn't much I could tell him about us that he hadn't heard before. He was familiar with our product, and he knew our story well. He understood that our label stood for something special in our industry. We built a brand by signing up farmers as franchisees, and we allowed them to stamp their eggs with our logo but only on the condition that they abided by our high standards. We were able to sign up the best farmers because Eggland's Best eggs could bring in an extra dollar over what generic eggs sold for. That's because the hens that produce our eggs are on all-vegetarian feed with no animal fats and with supplements such as kelp and rice bran. This special diet produces an egg lower in cholesterol and saturated fats that is also higher in Omega-3 fatty acids. At previous meetings I had shown him many studies to support these findings. I had presented surveys that revealed that our eggs taste better. And this buyer knew that many of his customers would only buy our eggs. I had gone over all of this before, and while he always agreed with me, the orders he placed were nowhere near the potential they should have been. "What can I do," I kept asking myself, "to increase the business we do with them to the next level?"

While I sat in the reception area waiting to meet with him, I kept thinking about what I could say to excite him and result in a bigger order. The buyer knew as well as I that we had a superior product. Time

SUCCESS SECRETS OF SALES SUPERSTARS

and time again I told him that Eggland's Best rejects more than 300,000 eggs every day that don't meet our standards. He had heard my pitch so many times that I knew none of the "same old" was going to excite him. If I didn't come up with something different, I could anticipate that the results would not be different. I kept thinking about what I could say to turn him on so he would increase what had become a standard order he placed with me. Then it dawned on me. I would try something different that I believed would work.

I walked into his office filled with enthusiasm, which I'm sure was a result of having convinced myself that what I would tell him would generate a bigger order.

We sat down at a small conference table, and I said, "Herb, let me start out by apologizing to you."

"What for?" he asked. "You haven't done anything wrong. You don't owe me an apology."

"But I do," I replied. "I've been calling on you for five years, and I have done a terrible job.

"Not true," he volunteered. "I think you've done a terrific job. There is no reason for you to be so hard on yourself."

"Let me show you why I've done such a poor job," I said. I took out a sheet of paper and wrote down some numbers that showed the business we did with other grocery chains. "Now look at the sales increases they've enjoyed over the years."

I let him look at the numbers before I continued. "Now here's what your company has done." Again I wrote down the numbers for the last five years and showed him that the business we did with his company was flat, though his competition had significant increases for the last five years.

After he studied the numbers for a minute or two, I said, "Their businesses have grown with us, but yours hasn't. Shame on me, Herb. It's my fault. I feel that I let you down."

While he was studying the numbers, I took out a blank check from my briefcase, and I said, "Here's what I'm willing to do. I will give you a check for $1 million that I guarantee will be your profits if you increase your business to this figure." And I pointed to the sheet of paper with a number written down.

"This $1 million is what your profit will be during the next 12 months, and I will write you a check for $1 million because I know this is how much your company will make."

"You'll guarantee me a million dollars?" he exclaimed.

"Exactly," I said, "if you'll give us this amount of your egg business during the next 12 months, I will put it in writing that you'll make a minimum of $1 million."

I felt comfortable offering him a $1 million profit because I knew that his company would actually make between $1.4 million and $1.5 million based on the numbers I asked him to commit to over the next 12 months. I calculated that he'd be making 25 cents per carton, but telling him I could guarantee him 25 cents a dozen wouldn't have had nearly the same impact that $1 million had.

Two weeks later, I met with the buyer, and this time his replenishment manager accompanied him. The buyer said, "Listen to Steve's proposal."

When I finished, he was apologetic. I told him, "No, no, no, it's not your fault. It's my fault because we haven't given you the help and the tools to make this work. We are here to make you look good. We are bringing in a new person. His entire job is going to be taking over this ordering function for you. And as a result, you will go from bad numbers that we've created to good numbers."

"Wow, this is great," the replenishment manager said. "I can't wait to do this."

I walked out of his office with an order significantly larger than any previous one ever placed with the company. Over the course of the year, his company's profits on Eggland's Best eggs well exceeded $1 million, and everyone was pleased.

The $1 million check proposal worked so well that I made up a mock overblown cardboard $1 million check that I used as a sales prop on other calls. We go in and say, "Here, this is for you," then we say, "Now this is what you have to do."

⋆ Barry's and Bob's Comments ⋆

Michella wasn't satisfied with getting the same results year after year and decided to do something different to get a bigger order. We like the way he apologized to his customer by telling him that he was to blame for the lack of increased sales over the past five years in comparison to how the competition fared. A lesser salesperson might have challenged the buyer and by doing so risked upsetting him. Wisely, he put the blame on himself and allowed the customer to save face. Then, rather than making the replenishment manager look bad, Michella again took the blame for the lack of increases in sales volume. In both instances, by blaming himself, the buyer and the replenishment manager insisted that it wasn't his fault.

We also salute Michella for being well prepared prior to making his presentation. He knew the customer's numbers as well as the competition's numbers. This enabled him to make comparisons that clearly demonstrated to the customer what his profits would be. These were relatively easy numbers for Michella to forecast. And as he points out in his story, $1 million profits sounds a lot bigger than a 25-cents-per-dozen profit! We also like Michella's sales prop. The cardboard check made payable to a customer for a large sum of money is something that you can emulate in your business. It is visual and makes a bold statement that will clearly make your point.

28

The Price of Happiness

Janis Spindel

Founder, CEO, Janis Spindel Serious Matchmaking Inc.

★ ★ ★

anis Spindel is president and founder of Janis Spindel Serious Matchmaking Inc., headquartered in New York City. She specializes in pairing upscale clientele she describes as "highly successful, well-educated, sophisticated, attractive professionals," some of whom are public figures and celebrities. Spindel's fees range from $50,000 to $500,000. She has a gift for matching people and was motivated to start her company in 1993 when she realized that 14 introductions she'd made resulted in matrimony in a one-year period.

Prior to starting her firm in 1993, she was in the fashion industry, representing French Maid, Poupee! and Colave for 15 years. In *this capacity, Spindel was in charge of sales throughout the U.S. She was also the proprietor of a retail company, Mommy and Me, which consisted of nine stores in the Tri-State area. Spindel is the best-known matchmaker in the U.S. and has appeared on many national TV shows, including* The CBS Early Show, The NBC Weekend Show, 60 Minutes II, Dr. Phil, The Today Show, The O'Reilly Factor, *and* Fox and Friends. *Spindel has been written about in many publications, including* The Wall Street Journal, New York *magazine,* The New York Times, *and* Fortune. *She is the author of two bestselling books,* Get Serious About Getting Married *and* How to Date Men. *She is involved in multiple charities and charitable events including The Libby Ross Foundation, Susan G. Komen Foundation, City Meals on Wheels, and St. Jude Hospital. She attended the University of Maryland. As of this writing, Spindel's matchmaking has resulted in 989 marriages.*

★ ★ ★

Matchmaking is a confidential business, so while my story is true I will use first names only and not reveal any client's identity

My clientele are men only. About 15 years ago I represented women, but I stopped because they are too needy. They are too high maintenance and have selective hearing. I meet 1,000-plus women a month, so I have a large selection of phenomenal women to match with my male clients. I am very selective—the women are well-educated, well-groomed, upscale, professional, nonsmoking, athletically inclined, commitment-minded, and attractive. I pride myself in the women I meet. Because the men are my clients, they pay the fee, not the women.

Many clients are referred to me by satisfied clients, plus I am constantly meeting people who know what I do, and they refer good prospects to me. My girlfriend Louise gave me Steve's name. He is a corporate attorney with a major New York City law firm. I called to tell him what I do, and he was intrigued. "Sounds interesting," he said. "What's the first step?"

"Before I take on a client, I go on a simulated date with him," I said. "Between asking him a lot of questions and scrutinizing what I observe, I am able to size him up. And after I get to know him, I am able to determine who's a good match for him."

"Makes sense," he said. "How does this simulated date work?"

"You and I will meet for either lunch or dinner. It will be like a date. In this environment I'll get to know you, and vice versa. I'll be observing your dating behaviors and considering with whom I think you will be compatible. I want to understand your wants and needs."

We met at an upscale restaurant. Steve was a tall, nice-looking bald man who wore glasses. He was a well-educated gentleman and dressed in a navy-blue suit. In the beginning, our conversation was mainly small talk, which is what I wanted because that's what couples typically do on a first date. We ordered a glass of wine and our dinner. Then we asked each other a lot of questions. I already had a profile on Steve so I knew the basics about him. I knew he was 45 years old and divorced, didn't have children, lived in New Jersey, worked at a major law firm in the City, and had graduated from an Ivy League school.

"As you know, I was married once," he volunteered. "We tried for eight years but didn't have children. For whatever reason, I don't know if it was her fault or mine, but it did have an effect on our marriage."

"I'm sorry, but those things happen," I said. It didn't take me long to know that Steve was a fabulous man, a truly good person. We had an excellent rapport which I consider a big plus. He was easy to talk to and a good listener.

"Do you date much?"

"It depends on how you define 'much,'" he smiled. I liked his smile.

"When we were first divorced, people were constantly fixing me up on dates, but not so much anymore. I enjoyed going on dates but after a while, I got tired of it. You know, all the small talk that people do on first dates. I realize that comes with the territory, but it can get boring."

"Only when you are with an uninteresting woman," I assured him. "The woman I will introduce to you will definitely not be boring."

"What makes you so sure?" he asked.

"I am very good at what I do," I replied. "I have a gift for matching people. I've matched hundreds of couples who got married. This is why I receive substantial fees for my service. I have a database of fabulous women, all of whom I have personally met, and they are exceptional. These are women you would not normally meet. That's because you're very busy at your law profession. Besides, you have a limited circle of contacts to make these introductions. I have access to so many wonderful women. As your matchmaker, I will become your eyes, your ears, your legs. I will leave no stone unturned until I find the right match for you. I'm out meeting women all day long and so is my staff. I have 25 women who are also scouting for me."

"I've had my share of bad blind dates," Steve said. "How do I know you'll match me up with the right woman?"

I asked him what he was looking for, and he gave me the criteria he wanted in his future wife. I politely listened but, for the most part, I already knew what he wanted. I own the minds of men. "Of course, she has to be attractive," he said, "and with a great body."

"Of course," I said. "Isn't that what all men want?"

"Yes, I suppose so," he said somewhat sheepishly.

"I like your honesty, Steve," I said, "and don't take this personally, but men are very visual and can be extremely superficial and shallow. It's part of their DNA. I know men want their women to be drop-dead gorgeous and sexy. And I'm not downplaying the importance of a physical attraction. There has to be chemistry, or it's a bad match. Men fall in love with their eyes. Don't worry, I will find somebody that you'll be attracted to. But then, Steve, there is the rest of the package as well."

He smiled and said, "How much information will I be given about the woman before I meet her?"

"I'll give you a profile on her, age, occupation, religion, and education, and yes, you'll get to see a photograph. At the same time, she will be given little information about you. Just your first name, your occupation, age, religion, but no photo."

"That's it?"

"Yes. Remember, you're my client, and she isn't. We don't want a woman to Google a man and be counting his money before she meets him. Remember, I have some clients who are billionaires and high-profile show business people. I have to protect my clients' privacy."

"I understand that your clients are successful, and I'm always concerned about running into gold diggers. Should I be with your matches?"

"As far as I know, that's never been a problem. I thoroughly screen the women. This is part of my service. I know what to look for and can spot a lot of things that a man won't see."

"How many clients do you typically work with at one time?" he asked.

"I don't count my clients," I answered. "You will always be on my radar screen."

"What if the chemistry isn't there?" he asked.

"That's an unknown quantity," I told him. "I will find attractive women, but the right chemistry is an unknown factor. After the first date, I expect both parties to call me. I want their feedback. It's interesting that 15 percent of my clients do marry their first introduction. But on average, it's between their third and sixth match."

"Impressive," he said and blurted out, "How much is the fee?"

"I require $50,000 upfront and when a match is one year old, I am paid another $50,000."

"Wow!" he said, "you are expensive."

"You're a highly paid attorney and are paid big fees. Your time is very valuable. Think of this as outsourcing work to a professional, someone who is much better than you at finding the right woman for you."

"You are right about that," he said. "I've not done well on my own. The truth is, I'm working such long hours at my law practice, I don't have time. Besides, the women that I do date are not what I'm looking for."

"Doing it the way you are, you might never meet the right woman."

"I understand what you will do for me, but $50,000 upfront is a lot of money. What makes you think you'll find the right match for me?"

"I don't take people if I think I can't deliver what they are looking for."

"Still, $50,000 . . ."

"It's simple," I said. "Men who want the Rolls Royce of matchmaking come to me."

"How do I know I'll get my money's worth?"

"Steve, you know that there are no guarantees in life. I can't guarantee to anyone that he'll be marching down the aisle. I don't know if a person is actually competent to get down the aisle. But what I can guarantee you is that I will work as hard as I can and I will leave no stone unturned until I deliver what you are asking for. The rest is up to chemistry and the universe. What I can guarantee you is that I will work for you day and night. I'll travel across the country, and I will find a match for you."

"It sounds good," he said, hesitantly. "But $50,000 . . ."

"I understand your concern," I said, "and you're not the first client to get sticker shock. But keep in mind what I do is priceless. My fee is a small price to pay to be happy for the rest of your life."

"I agree," he said. "I have some friends who married the wrong woman, and they paid dearly for their mistakes. It can run into the millions."

"So what are you waiting for?" I told him. "Be like Nike. Just do it."

He nodded. I looked him in the eye and said, "I will send you a contract to read. Sign it and return it to me with a check for $50,000. Once I get it, I'll set up an appointment to do a home visit."

"A home visit?" he asked.

"A man's home is his castle," I said, "so I go to my client's home and, if needed, I make suggestions on what needs to be done. For instance, a very wealthy man who also lived in New Jersey had a home that couldn't have been colder. It reminded me of a Four Seasons or Peninsula Hotel. It was just plain sterile. My image team came out to work on it and gave it some warmth."

After dinner, Steve thanked me for my time. Two days later I received a signed agreement and a check from him.

I liked Steve, and I had a perfect match for him. Her name was Amanda. She was a schoolteacher. She was quite attractive and had a great figure, but she didn't have movie star looks. I knew instantaneously that they were perfect for each other. When I met with her to set up their first date, I told her, "Amanda, do you want to know who you are going to marry?" She looked at me like I had lost it. I told her about Steve. Amanda and Steve had their first date, and they both called the next day to say how well it went. They were married by the end of year. They have two children, a boy and a girl. They are very much in love and couldn't be happier.

⋆ Barry's and Bob's Comments ⋆

Janis Spindel is recognized as America's number-one matchmaker. She deals with an exclusive clientele, and yes, her fees are pricey. But as she points out, she performs a priceless service, one that she explains "is a small price to pay to be happy for the rest of your life." Of course, it's not for everyone—only a small percentage of people can afford it. But then, only an affluent person can afford to buy expensive artwork or a sizable flawless diamond. For the unique service Spindel offers and the happiness it brings to a satisfied client, we believe what she delivers is well worth the price. After all, what is more valuable than one's happiness?

We applaud the way she confidently explained the cost of her service, and didn't hesitate to close the sale at the right time. When her client questioned the cost and expressed several times that it was high, Spindel wasn't distracted or dismayed; she gave him reasons why it was worth the price. She did it like a true professional. Why? Because she strongly believed that she could deliver what she was offering—and she did.

Spindel also understands that successful people place a high value on their time. She realizes that her busy clients don't have the time to meet desirable women, so she does it for them. Knowing this, she caters to their need to maximize what their time is worth, and paying for her services and the happiness it will bring is money well spent.

29

The Sale That Saved the World's Biggest-Selling Drug

Roger Newton

Co-Discoverer of Lipitor

★ ★ ★

Roger Newton is the co-discoverer of Lipitor, the world's top-selling drug, which reduces LDL cholesterol. Lipitor had peak annual sales of $13 billion in 2006, making it the highest-selling drug in the world, more than double the second leading drug. In a period of 22 years, its sales exceeded $100 billion. During his 17-year tenure at Warner-Lambert/Parke-Davis, which later became a wholly owned subsidiary of Pfizer, Newton served as chairman of the Atherosclerosis Discovery Team for 12 years.

In 1998, one year after Lipitor received FDA approval and was launched in the market, Newton left Pfizer and founded Esperion Therapeutics Inc., a biopharmaceutical company. The *new enterprise's mission was to discover and develop pharmaceutical products to treat cardiovascular diseases through the use of HDL Therapy, a new approach that focused on infusions of synthetic HDL or high-density lipoprotein to regress atherosclerosis in people with heart disease.*

A lipid biochemist for more than 30 years, Newton's research interests have centered on the nutritional and pharmacological regulation of cholesterol and lipoprotein metabolism as they relate to atherosclerosis and vascular diseases. In 2004, after five years as an independent company, Esperion was acquired by Pfizer for $1.3 billion, and Newton was working again with some of his former employees as senior vice president and director. In May 2008 Newton and a group of investors raised $23 million to purchase former Esperion patents, as well as the name Esperion Therapeutics to restart the company. Newton currently serves as the company's president and CEO.

The same year that Esperion was acquired by Pfizer, he and his wife, Coco, put 25 percent of the personal gross proceeds they received from the sale into the Esperance Family Foundation. Their family-run organization supports nonprofit organizations with a focus on human potential, social justice, health, and the environment. In 2005, the family foundation made a multiyear financial commitment to Golden Courage International, an organization based in Beijing and Ann Arbor, Michigan. GCI provides educational programs and services to Chinese children who have been affected and/or orphaned by AIDS and other maladies. Newton has served as GCI's chairman since 2005.

In the mid-1980s, I was chairman of the atherosclerosis discovery team at Parke-Davis. At the time, my co-chairman was Bruce Roth, a brilliant synthetic chemist, who is recognized as the inventor of Lipitor. Over a period of six years, Bruce and I worked on 20 different chemical series. With each series, we looked at many different compounds to discover the best ones we could put forward as a lead compound for further development. Bruce focused on the chemical synthesis and I was responsible for overseeing the function of the biological side, which was to screen the compounds for inhibitory activity to reduce cholesterol synthesis.

Roth and his team of chemists were turning out one compound after another. All of these compounds were then tested by my team of biologists. When a particular compound showed promise, it was reviewed and discussed by the biologists and then sent back to the chemists, and together the atherosclerosis discovery team discussed the recommendations that would be made for further evaluation. It was the highest performing team I've ever been on. Everyone knew his or her role on this team and everyone knew our number-one goal, which was the discovery of a potent compound to inhibit cholesterol synthesis and lower LDL. I attribute this to the fact that we assembled a group of people with different expertise that complemented each other and allowed each team member to stay focused on his or her own task without having to be concerned about what others were doing.

During the many years we spent to discover and develop a statin drug, our team concentrated on coming up with ideas to make a better drug than the competition. We studied what the other companies were doing and searched for ways to make improvements and, more importantly, to have a potent and superior compound for the lowering of LDL cholesterol. In time, we came up with the idea that we could make a statin that was tissue selective, meaning that the compound was taken up more by the liver but rejected by other tissues. The approach led us to realize that because the blood circulates from the intestines and goes to the liver, we could then potentially find a liver-specific compound. Knowing this, we asked, "What happens if the liver was effective at taking up the compound and very little of the drug actually got into circulation?" We concluded that would be the equivalent of tissue selectivity and chose atorvastatin, in part for this reason. This would be our ticket to making an effective statin in humans, which controls the cholesterol pathway in the liver by inhibiting the HMG-CoA reductase, the rate of living enzyme for cholesterol synthesis.

During the early 1980s in the preliminary stages of our statin program, it was not known if it was possible to make a cholesterol medicine that would be truly safe. By this time, Sankyo had toxicology problems with compactin and discontinued its development program. Undeterred, we developed a chemical series that possessed penta-substituted pyrroles. It contained the compound that was the structural pattern followed by all of the other statin compounds. While it showed promise, it was necessary to prove that CI–981 did not have toxicity problems similar to earlier compounds. The code name CI–981 stands for a compound currently undergoing "clinical investigation." Having a CI number was significant because it meant the compound had tested well in numerous screens and assays which produced a desired pharmacological profile. Having passed these tests, the compound was advanced to determine if it worked to inhibit cholesterol synthesis to lower LDL cholesterol in preclinical models. Most compounds that get failing grades for further development are identified only by a PD number and were tightly sealed for storage and destined to spend an eternity on a shelf somewhere in a remote company compound library. Thousands of screened compounds have this fate.

For example, an earlier compound that showed promise was numbered PD123,588, but when a similar compound was patented by a Sandoz chemist, it was terminated. We had four lead compounds in the pyrrole series before CI–981 (atorvastatin calcium). Two tested toxic, a cause for much gloom and doom for our team. It was now 1988 and years of research had been put into our statin program, and at this point, CI–981 was our only viable candidate. If it also proved toxic, our team that had worked for six years on our pyrrole series would have no choice but to either start from scratch or terminate our efforts altogether to develop a statin drug. CI–981 was definitely our only compound to develop and was given the generic name atorvastatin calcium. With favorable results from tests in preclinical models, our team was ready to move forward and test CI-981's efficacy and safety in human clinical trials.

However, the preclinical tests showed that atorvastatin calcium was more potent but not significantly more effective in lowering LDL. It had just a bit better effect on triglycerides in some models.

Prior to being acquired by Pfizer, Parke-Davis was a mid-tier pharmaceutical company with limited resources. To many company executives, it would be tantamount to throwing good money after bad to continue work on atorvastatin. What would be the point in doing clinical tests on humans? The costs of testing it on humans would potentially run into the hundreds of millions of dollars.

I refused to throw in the towel. We had put so much time and effort into our statin program, and everyone knew that the preclinical models are not conclusive, because tests on humans might potentially give better results. To my way of thinking, it made perfectly good sense to take it to the next level and do a Phase I clinical study. Unlike a full-blown clinical development plan, this study would involve a small number of humans and wouldn't be outrageously expensive.

The naysayers argued, "Too little, too late." The marketing people were most vocal. "Without a competitive advantage," they insisted, "we won't be able to sell it, so it has no potential commercial viability." Without the support of marketing, it appeared that the atorvastatin program had run its course.

In a last-ditch attempt to gain support, I made an appeal to Ronald Cresswell, chairman and chief scientific officer at Parke-Davis' pharmaceutical research division. Reminding my boss that the company had already invested considerable time and effort, I said, "Let's spend another million to see how it works on humans. Bruce and I are convinced it will lower LDL cholesterol even in healthy volunteers. Please, Ron, go along with our team's decision."

Cresswell listened intently and understood that the real test on safety and tolerability comes from testing in people. He agreed to take it to a review board, a committee that would have 12 senior leaders in attendance. The review board's decision would be final.

"We will listen with an open mind," Cresswell said, "but we will only approve a medicine when we are convinced that the science being presented was sufficiently predictive of its commercial viability."

The members of the committee needed to have a certain comfort level with the potential pharmacologic benefit in humans with the new drug, or they would veto it.

Bruce Roth and I waited in a small room outside the meeting room where I would make a do-or-die presentation. All the hard work of our colleagues on the statin program over the past six years depended on the outcome of my presentation. Bruce and I agreed that I would present it to the review committee.

It was a formal meeting, and the members of the review committee understood they were there to prudently make an important decision. Just before I got up to speak, I leaned over to Bruce and said in a hushed whisper, "Don't worry, Bruce, I'm not going to let management kill atorvastatin for no good reason."

I began my presentation by thanking the committee members for their attendance and consideration of an important decision that I believed could very well define the future of the company. I reminded them about how much hard work had been put into the statin program by many highly committed and dedicated employees. I then talked about the preclinical tests and reiterated that the results of efficacy and safety justified further development.

At this point in the presentation, there wasn't much of a reaction. Sensing that I wasn't winning over my audience, I thought that unless I did something dramatic, I was fighting a losing battle. At that moment, I recalled something that my wife Coco had said to me at 3 a.m. that morning, when I was having a sleepless night and had awakened her. Her advice was that I should do something dramatic at the meeting to capture their attention and to dispel their concerns.

"If not," Coco said, "they will simply pass on it like they are so accustomed to doing with the vast majority of compounds they review." I listened to her suggestion but paid no heed to it until now, when it was time to present it to the committee.

Suddenly, I found myself getting down on one knee and pleading to the committee members. "You've got to let us do the human tests," I said, flinging my arms above my head. "I know it's the right thing to do, and I'm begging you to do it."

It was as if I was doing an Al Jolson imitation, and I realized at that moment that if I really got their attention, it would change the momentum of the meeting. Only then, I thought, they might be more open to listen to what I had to say.

Previously, the tension in the air was so thick you could cut it with a knife. My hamming it up caught them off guard. At first, it made them fidget and nobody said a word. Then a smile appeared on someone's face, and then another, and another. The smiles were followed by laughter. At that point I knew they were now willing to hear my story. I laughed to let them know I wasn't actually on my knees begging. What they realized was that I possessed so much passion and conviction that I was willing to risk making a fool of myself to make my point.

When the room quieted down, I told them in earnest, "We showed that we can lower LDL in preclinical models. We know that it inhibited cholesterol synthesis and it affected the enzyme in the way we wanted it to. Now let's find out exactly how good it is with humans. We've come this far and this is not the time to throw in the towel."

The committee consented to grant its approval for atorvastatin to go forward and have it tested in humans.

The first test consisted of 24 Warner-Lambert employees who volunteered to take Lipitor. Unlike most drugs, it only took a couple of weeks of carefully monitoring volunteers to find out if atorvastatin lowered LDL cholesterol. At 10 milligrams, LDL dropped more than 30 percent, which was equal to or better than competing compounds at their recommended maximum doses. At 80 milligrams, LDL dropped 58 percent—about 40 percent more than the competition. It cost the company about $1 million to conduct the Phase I test on the 24 patients. The Phase II and Phase III clinical trials would run into the hundreds of millions of dollars, involving thousands of people and taking several years to complete. It was an excellent investment that over the years returned billions of dollars in profits for both Warner-Lambert/Parke-Davis and Pfizer. Most importantly, atorvastatin (Lipitor) was shown to delay or prevent heart attacks in millions of people around the world by reducing their bad cholesterol.

★ Barry's and Bob's Comments ★

With the results from the test on the first 24 humans, the company made the decision to make a huge investment on a considerably larger population. Had Newton not made his passionate presentation to the review board, the world's all-time biggest-selling drug would have never happened. However, Newton emphasizes, "The key to convincing the review board was based on great science more than my salesmanship." Substance always takes precedent over salesmanship. Having said this, failing to have good salesmanship may result in quality products, services, and ideas getting passed over and never being commercialized for the benefit of humanity.

Imagine standing in front of a review board attended by sophisticated pharmaceutical executives and scientists who routinely reject far more drugs than they approve. This is what Newton faced when he made his presentation to the committee members who would determine whether the company would move forward with atorvastatin, the medicine now known as Lipitor. There was a lot at stake with the outcome of the committee's decision. If it vetoed the drug, years of research and hard work would have been wasted. It would have been devastating to Newton, Roth, and their co-workers. As the person responsible for making the presentation to the committee, Newton was under considerable pressure to make the sale. He relied on showmanship and his sense of humor to make his point. No one had ever made such an unconventional presentation to the company's review committee. Newton's resourcefulness saved the day—and, it could be said, contributed to saving the lives of millions of Lipitor patients around the world.

We salute Newton's stalwart performance under extreme pressure and mentioned to him how unusual it was for a man with his scientific background to possess his selling skills. He smiled and confided to us, "For two summers while I was in college I worked 80 hours a week selling educational books for the Southwestern Publishing Company, a publisher based in Nashville, Tennessee. The first summer I went door-to-door in small towns in Indiana, and the second summer I sold books in small communities in upstate New York. This sales background has served me well over the years. I say this having seen other scientists with good ideas that never see the light of day because they don't know how to sell those ideas." We concur. Newton's story demonstrates that everyone sells, but those who know how to sell with conviction enjoy a huge advantage over those who don't.

Be Flexible

Hal Becker

Sales/Customer Service Consultant

★ ★ ★

Hal Becker, founder and CEO of The Becker Group, is an internationally-known expert on sales, customer service, and negotiating. Based in Solon, Ohio, he is a dynamic speaker who makes more than 140 presentations a year. His impressive list of clients includes IBM, Disney, New York Life, Blue Cross, AT&T, Pearle Vision, and Cintas, as well as hundreds of other companies and associations.

After graduating from John Carroll University in Cleveland with a bachelor's degree in sociology in 1976, Becker worked for Xerox Corporation, and at age 22 he was the company's number-one salesperson among a national sales force of 11,000. In 1983, he launched

Direct Opinions, one of America's first customer service telemarketing firms. He sold the company in 1990 to devote himself full time to consulting and presenting lectures around the world.

Becker is a syndicated writer in 46 business journal newspapers nationwide. He is the author of four books, Can I Have 5 Minutes of Your Time? At Your Service, Lip Service, *and* Get What You Want!

Becker has received many honors, including being only one of eight people to receive the Toastmasters International Communication and Leadership Award. Inc. *magazine voted Becker one of the nation's top speakers in the areas of sales and customer service. In 2010, Salesgurus. net voted Becker one of the world's top 30 professional sales trainers.*

A cancer survivor, Becker founded the Cancer Hotline, a non-profit organization to which he donates the proceeds of his books. He is a past chairman of his local Chamber of Commerce and has served as a trustee on the following boards: Better Business Bureau of Cleveland, March of Dimes, Council of Smaller Enterprises, University of Akron Business School, Cleveland Health Museum/ Natural History Museum, Healthy Cities Ohio, and the Montefiore Nursing Home.

★ ★ ★

A little over a year ago, I received a call from the sales manager at HDT Global, a company based in my hometown, Solon, Ohio. I had met the company's CEO on the golf course, talked briefly to him, and gave him my business card. He told his sales manager to book me for a speaking engagement at a conference to be held in Virginia. HDT specializes in designing and manufacturing a host of products used by the militaries of the U.S. and its allies. The company's product line includes shelters, power generators, heaters, environmental control units, and air filtration equipment deployed by the military worldwide. A high percentage of the HDT sales force has a military background.

The company checked me into a local Hampton Inn that was close to my speaking gig. The next morning I planned on delivering an inspirational, content-driven speech, one that I have given many times before to other sales forces. The morning of my speech, the sales manager called me at my hotel room. He was friendly enough. He inquired about my trip to Virginia and asked, "Did you get a good night's sleep, Hal?"

"I did," I replied, "and I'm looking forward to my meeting with your sales force."

"I wouldn't if I were you," he replied.

"Did you just say that if you were I, you wouldn't look forward to speaking to your sales organization today?"

"That's right, Hal," he said. "Our guys absolutely hated the two previous speakers we brought in. You are probably going to bomb, too. But we had to have someone here, so that's you. Anyhow, see you in a little while, and good luck today."

When I walked down the hall for breakfast, I couldn't help but notice one of their sales reps running up and down the hall doing wind sprints. He was dressed in green fatigues. I saw a lot of macho guys in the eating area, and I could tell from their posture and haircuts that they were ex-army personnel and Marines. At breakfast I found out that HDT had a practice of hiring ex-military people who were a good fit with their corporate culture.

I arrived at the meeting room early and listened to the speaker I would follow. He talked about installing lighting equipment in military shelters that HDT set up in the field. Everyone listened intently, and they all participated in asking a lot of questions. They were completely engaged in what he told them. The speaker was an ex-military man, and his audience identified with him. I didn't have a military background, and I felt that I was completely out of my element.

When I was introduced, I noticed how the sales reps sat back in their seats. I could see from their body language that they weren't looking forward to my speech. I spoke for about 10 minutes and knew I was losing my audience. They were squirming in their seats, looking at their watches, and some were yawning. I've spoken thousands of times, and I know when I have my audience and when I don't. This audience was clearly not with me.

In frustration, I stopped talking, and after a long, silent pause, I said, "Okay, guys, here's the deal. We have a long day ahead of us. I am going to talk for 20 more minutes, and then I'm going to take a 20-minute break. I'm going to leave you all while I make a few phone calls. During my absence, I want you to discuss whether you want me to continue with the six-hour workshop I've been paid to do. From what my gut is telling me, the response I'm receiving from you is that you're not exactly thrilled that I'm here today."

I caught them by surprise. There was a hush in the room. "If you decide you don't want me to conduct the workshop, you won't hurt my feelings. You know how it goes. Some people like vanilla ice cream, and some like chocolate. I won't take it personally. The one thing I don't want is to waste my day with you. Nor do you want to waste your day with me. If you decide you don't want me, I won't send an invoice to the company, and I'll pay for my airfare. So it won't cost HDT anything.

"If you decide that you want me to come back, we'll finish the day. But in order for it to work, we have to partner up on this. I will make a promise to you that the day will fly by. We'll have fun. And you will learn stuff that you forgot about selling and what it takes to be a pro. I say this knowing that there is nothing new in sales. What I will talk about are the four reasons why salespeople fail. Number one, you must like what you do. If you get up every day and say, 'This job sucks,' you are not going to do well. Number two, I know as ex-military people, you understand how to get on a military base where a civilian like I cannot. But you've got to see the right decision maker. I'll tell you how to do that. Number three, in addition to making calls on your existing customers on a base, you have to know how to sell multiple customers and spend your entire day on that base.

Number four, many salespeople fail because they are doing what I am doing right now: They talk too much. They don't ask questions. Okay, I'm out of here. I'll be back in 20 minutes to find out if you want me to continue or go home."

I spent 20 minutes in my rented car making phone calls, and then I went back to the conference room. When I walked in, they gave me a round of applause, and I spent the rest of the day addressing a very receptive audience, and in fact, one of my all-time favorites.

☆ Barry's and Bob's Comments ☆

Becker says that the lesson from his story is that a salesperson must address his customer's needs, not what he or she wants to sell. A salesperson must be flexible and realize that not all customers or, in Becker's case, audiences are identical. "When I was told, 'The guys aren't going to like you,'" Becker explains, "I surmised that if I didn't make some adjustments, I would bomb. I also knew that my audience was ex-military, which meant it didn't need to hear me talk about discipline. Nor did it need to hear me tell them about honor or respect. It already had those qualities. I understood that like other salespeople, they wanted to make money and they wanted to enjoy their jobs. By understanding my audience (customer), I was able to save the day."

We admire Becker's upfront approach. He didn't mince words when he said that he wasn't interested in wasting anyone's time—his or theirs. Yes, he risked losing his speaking fee, which most speakers would not be willing to do, and we believe this is what got their attention and won their admiration. When customers see that a salesperson's motivation is not simply his paycheck, they are more receptive to what he has to say. Had Becker been inflexible and stuck to his prepared presentation, it is probable that he would have failed. Certainly, we believe that a salesperson must have a well-prepared sales presentation, but having said this, he or she must also be prepared to be flexible and go with the flow.

Building a Strong Company Culture

Shau-wai Lam

Chairman of the Board, DCH Auto Group

★ ★ ★

*S*hau-wai Lam is the Chairman of the Board of DCH Auto Group, one of the largest automobile dealership companies in the U.S. Based in South Amboy, New Jersey, DCH owns and operates 29 automobile dealerships, including those for Acura, Audi, BMW, Chrysler, Dodge, Honda, Jeep, Kia, Lexus, Nissan, Scion, and Toyota, located in New Jersey, New York, Connecticut, and California. When Shau-wai joined the company in 1967, DCH was the Dah Chong Hong Trading Corporation, headquartered in Hong Kong, a company founded in the late 1930s by his father, B. Y. Lam, in Shanghai. The U.S. subsidiary initially specialized in commodity trading and the importation of food and clothing.

In 1977, DCH (USA) shifted its focus to automobiles and opened its first dealership, DCH Paramus Honda, in New Jersey. In 1979, Shau-wai was sent to Los Angeles to launch DCH's Western Region. He was responsible for the startup of DCH Gardena Honda and DCH Tustin Acura; both became the top national ranking dealerships of their respective franchises under his leadership. Shau-wai became president of DCH in 1988. When the Hong Kong parent company was acquired by another company in 1992, the Lam family and the Wing On Group of Hong Kong jointly acquired the American subsidiary. Shau-wai became president of DCH in 1988.

Retail sales are within reach of the $2 billion. Over the years, the company has received numerous awards from its franchisors as well as industrywide honors. No other auto group has received as many of the prestigious J.D. Power and Associates Dealer of Excellence Awards, a recognition presented for achieving the highest honor in customer satisfaction. In 2004 Shau-wai received the Time *magazine Quality Dealer Award for New Jersey, the 2004 National Association of Minority Automobile Dealers' Lifetime Achievement Award, the 2004 Champion of Life Award from GMAC, the 2005* Newsweek *magazine Dealer of the Year Finalist Award, and the 2005 Dealer of the Year Award from* Ward's Dealer Business *magazine. In 2007, Shau-wai was the recipient of the 2006 Ellis Island Medal of Honor and the Ernst & Young New Jersey Entrepreneur of the Year Award for Retail/Distribution Services. In 2008 he was the recipient of the U.S. Department of Commerce Certificate of Appreciation.*

Shau-wai is a graduate of Purdue University with B.S. and M.S. degrees in mathematics. He also has an M.B.A. from New York University. He received a Distinguished Science Alumnus Award from Purdue University in 2004. He serves as a director on the boards of

Directors of of National Automobile Dealers Charitable Foundation, National Association of Minority Automobile Dealers, Toyota-Lexus Minority Dealers Association, New Jersey Chinese-American Chamber of Commerce, and American Friends of the Shanghai Museum.

★ ★ ★

In the 1930s, my father, B. Y. Lam, started Dah Chong Hong Limited, a trading company in Shanghai. In Chinese, Dah Chong Hong means *Great Prosperous Company*. In retrospect, it was our vision, and ever since, we have been striving to advance towards that vision and the bar keeps rising. He believed that customers always came first and serving them was the company's top priority. It still is. But back in the 1930s, few businesspeople thought this way. Based on this business philosophy, my father built a very successful company, and the same core values were applied when he founded a bank in Hong Kong. That enterprise is now the Hang Seng Bank, which was later acquired by HSBC. Operating under my father's business philosophy, this bank became well-known for its exceptional customer service. Today, Hang Seng Bank ranks number two in local deposits among the hundreds of banks in Hong Kong.

In 1948, my father's trading company came to the U.S. to open a branch office in New York City. In 1977, we opened a Honda automobile dealership in Paramus, New Jersey, and two years later, I was sent to Los Angeles to open a DCH Honda dealership in Gardena, which became our beachhead in Southern California. In 1988, I was named president of the company, and three years later, the trading company was acquired by another company in Hong Kong. That's when my family and the Wing On Group of Hong Kong purchased the U.S. operations, and DCH Auto Group became a completely independent company.

We opened other dealerships, and by 1997, we had 20 located in New Jersey, New York, and California. Our dealerships represented different automobile companies and were spread out geographically. We had become a large company consisting of separate operating units. This prompted us to accurately define our company culture and heritage or we would risk losing it. That's because, at the time, we had nothing officially written about our company's values. It had always been passed down by word-of-mouth and by our actions. I felt that DCH was becoming too big to continue without a clearly defined mission statement that incorporated our core values. By putting it in writing, it would be uniformly known by all of our people; of course, its effectiveness would depend on how well it was implemented. This might not sound like a difficult task, but it was to us, especially when our company consisted of 20-plus separate units in different locations, each operating independently. To complicate matters our dealerships didn't want to lose their independence, nor did we want them to.

Our vision is actually expressed in our name, the Great Prosperous Company. Dah is great, Chong is prosperous and in Chinese, Hong means company. That's right—our vision is embedded in our name. We are confident that we can provide our customers with a good experience and our goal is to deliver customer happiness. To make this claim, we can only do it after we can consistently deliver that promise.

Back in 1997, our first step was to ask our senior managers to survey our team members at all levels throughout the organization. Then along with three senior executives, Billy Wong, Susan Scarola, and George Liang, we invited our senior managers and dealership general managers to a meeting in Mission Inn Resort in Orlando. During these meetings we worked on team building and conducted sessions to discuss our culture and values. By putting our heads together to identify our core values, we were able to develop our mission statement with these core values embedded in it.

Our goal was to be among the industry leaders. We would achieve this by building a large base of happy and loyal customers. To make our customers happy all the time, we must have happy employees. We believe in the power of the team being much stronger than the individual. And to have sustainable leadership, we must be innovative and build an impeccable reputation by conducting ourselves with honesty and integrity. Putting all these together, our Mission Statement was born: "To be an innovative industry leader, totally committed to customer satisfaction, employee satisfaction, integrity, and teamwork."

We also developed guiding principles using the acronym, TEAMDCH. An acronym makes it easy for our people to remember. T is *Trust*. We must earn trust. E is *Excellence*. We are always in pursuit of excellence. A is *Attitude*. We need to have a positive attitude because people with a negative attitude will fail. A positive attitude is required to succeed. M is *Mutual Respect,* which is essential for establishing good relationship. D is *Dedication*. We are dedicated to our mission and our core values. We are dedicated to make each of our dealerships, the dealership of choice for consumers, and also the company of choice to work for. C is *Communication*. Good communication is needed to build a good team as well as good customer relation. And H is *Honesty*. This is TEAMDCH.

Our mission and guiding principles are the same today as they were when Dah Chong Hong was founded in the 1930s. Our DCH heritage is a powerful foundation on which we build our future. Our principles for success remain the same: doing the right thing—for our customers, for each other, for our shareholders. We sincerely believe that the best way to do business is behaving with honesty, with integrity and with the highest ethical standards. This is how we will be well known as a reputable place to buy and service automobiles. We will stay in touch with and continue to delight our customers so that they will remain as our customers for life and recommend us to friends and family. Everything else is subject to change. Our organization, our people, our buildings, our products, our strategies may change. But our core values are unchanging.

We then came up with what we call *The DCH Way*. It would serve as a daily guide for our people to follow on how to treat customers and each other. To get it right, we engaged one of the best consultants in the world, Larry Light, who is credited as the brand marketer who helped to turn McDonald's brand image around in 2004 when the fast-food chain's business had been in decline.

I first met Light when he was a branding consultant for Nissan and I was very impressed with his presentation about the power of a strong brand. When I got reconnected with him in 2005, he was working full time for McDonald's as its Global Chief Marketing Officer. I thought there was little chance that we could engage him, but I tried to arouse his interest so that he would give me some good advice.

I explained to him that DCH had always focused on serving our customers and that's not just lip-service. Inspired by our Mission Statement and guiding principles, our team members put their hearts and souls behind this company heritage. That's how we differentiate ourselves from competition and we have earned a lot of recognition for our efforts. *Time* magazine named me the Time Quality Dealer Award recipient in New Jersey," I told him. "It was an honor to accept the award on behalf of the company because it was a team effort."

"That's a coincidence," Light said. "As a result of the work I did with McDonald's, I was selected as Marketer of the Year by *Brandweek* magazine." He went on to explain, "Automobile dealers in general have a low image and I'd like to help improve it. I think the marketer of the year and the dealer of the year can do something together that would make a difference.

"The timing is good because my work with McDonald's is about to complete," Light said. He then explained, "McDonald's wasn't giving its targeted customers the experience they expected to get. We revitalized the company's brand and marketing strategy and its customers are now getting that positive experience. Consequently, its customers are coming back and McDonald's is again very successful."

I said, "In comparison to McDonald's, we're a small company and while I would like you to help us, we cannot afford to pay what McDonald's can."

"I am sure we can come up with a price for my services that will be affordable," Larry said. Apparently, he found the project to be so challenging that money was not a major issue. The challenges were to overcome the legacy of poor image suffered by auto dealers and to establish a distinguish brand identity within the umbrella of a much more dominant brand of the manufacturer.

Light interviewed more than 100 people in the organization at all levels. He then assembled team members from each dealership department to form a brand strategy task force. Meeting five times during the development process, Larry helped the task force identify five key elements that we wanted our customers to feel. The first was WELCOME. We want the customer to feel welcome at our dealership. This goes beyond a greeting and a big smile. It includes such things as a welcoming environment, cleanliness, directional signs, and the appearance of our people. The second element was RESPECT. Many dealerships fail to respect their customers. This is especially true with female customers who commonly are apprehensive about shopping for a vehicle alone. They often ask a male companion to go along to help them. It was typical that when a man and woman came into a dealership, a salesperson was apt to greet the male companion first, and even though it was the woman who was buying the car, they directed their conversation to him, not her. And although when she asked a question, they tended to answer the question as if the man asked it. This treatment to women is disrespectful. We want our customers to feel respected. Salespeople traditionally can also be disrespectful to a young person. They assume that he or she can't qualify for credit and only after a few minutes with the prospect, they ask, "Where are your parents? Is your father going to co-sign?"

In addition to feeling respected, we want our customers to feel PRODUCTIVE. At competing dealerships, customers expressed that salespeople unnecessarily waste their time. People are very busy today. Our people value our customer's time. We also want our customers to feel CONFIDENT. We want them to have the comfort afterwards that they came to the right dealership and we will help them find the right vehicle or solution so after their purchase or servicing of their vehicle, they will have no regret. We don't want anyone to have buyer's remorse or doubts.

The fifth element is ENTHUSED. This comes from going beyond what customers can expect at other dealerships. When they do business with us, we want our customers to feel as if they have experienced a new discovery, something that is delightful. We want them to be so excited that they will tell their friends and family about it. When so, they will become our advocate.

The DCH Way is easy to understand and it was easy to convince everyone to believe in it. But it is a difficult task to execute it smoothly.

Of course it has to start at the top. As the chairman of the board, I visited every one of our dealerships with Susan Scarola, our CEO at the time and now our Vice Chairman, to launch The DCH Way. Susan and I, along with our regional managers went to our dealerships to explain our philosophy and we met with all of our team members. Because our stores are open long hours, there are different shifts of people so we had to do these sessions twice at each dealership we visited. It took us nearly two months to complete our launch at all of our dealerships. During these sessions, we explained our views and welcomed everyone's feedback. This gave them ownership in what we were doing. We emphasized to them that The DCH Way experience had to be delivered from our heart and soul. Before we could deliver it to our customer, our team members must receive the same five key experiences working at the company. Therefore, the same five key elements are how we want our team members to be treated and how they treat each other.

Furthermore, for everyone to be on the same page and make it work, it takes more than putting it on paper and talking about it now and then. For it to work, everyone must practice it day-in and day-out. This meant that we had to devise a way for it to be second-nature to them, so when one faces a moment-of-truth, it is natural for him or her to behave in the DCH Way. With five elements, we conduct a daily word-of-the-day session throughout the five-day workweek. For instance, on Monday, we talk about Welcome. Tuesday, the topic is Respect, and so on. We do this week after week in a brief morning session. Each week, we pair the word-of-the-day with one of the 7 Ps. These are seven areas where we can make improvements—Place, Product, People, Process, Price, Promotion, and Performance. Thus we have a 35-day cycle, so for a 7-week period, they talk about a different pairing each day. By letting team members know session topics in advance, they have time to think about it prior to the morning meeting and come prepared. Over time, through repetition, our people are able to form a clear understanding about the DCH Way because it becomes engrained in their thinking. During these 10–15 minute sessions, anyone can bring up success stories as well as anything that we need to improve on relating to the day's pairing, and together, along with some coaching, we may be able to solve the problem right away. If the problem requires longer discussion to resolve, it is referred to a task force.

Depending on the size of the store, we may have one or more task forces. Each task force, consists of representatives from each department. They meet each day for about half-an-hour to find solutions to problems that have been referred to it and to work on other improvement opportunities. Action plans are then developed with goals and timelines. They are posted and tracked in the company's internal website with progress updates. Members of the task force serve out a 7-week cycle period and then new members would come on board.

Each year, our President George Liang and I would make a special trip to each dealership to reinforce our team members' commitment to The DCH Way.

Bear in mind that we don't just talk about the DCH Way, we walk the talk. If we only talked about it, it would be theory, not reality. We demonstrate it by our actions. For example, we stress honesty and if a team member violates this core value, we will discuss it with him, coach him, and if it is a major offense or one that is repeated, he will be asked to leave our organization. It does not matter if the individual was a productive member, we will not tolerate dishonesty. This applies to everyone at all levels. For example, a general sales manager at one of our big dealerships was in violation of the DCH Way. We had many complaints from team members that he talked down to everyone and didn't treat them with respect. We had several conversations with him but he continued to disrespect team members. We had no choice but to ask him to leave.

At one dealership, a manager was falsifying information in order to receive incentives offered by an automaker. When we found out we immediately notified the automaker and we discharged the manager. In another incidence, in an internal audit, we discovered that a finance and insurance manager was falsifying the paperwork as well as customers' signatures on applications that were submitted to banks. In incidences when it was necessary to redo the paperwork, the manager did this as a matter of convenience. If our internal audit uncovers such violations, our policy is to notify the bank that information is not correct and to terminate the manager. When our people observe how the DCH Way is implemented, it becomes more than just a clever slogan written on a piece of paper.

We are quick to respond to customer complaints. George Liang and I lead by example. We promptly return calls or emails to customers, and most important, after they explain their dissatisfaction, we follow up with solutions. This demonstrates how we respect our customer and it instills confidence in customers that they are doing business with an honorable company.

In America, there is a lot of emphasis placed on winning. In sports, for example, winning is everything. However, in business, you could lose this time, but the customer will come back, and in the end, you both will be winners. In situations when you can't have two winners, we want the customer to win. As my father used to say, "Don't worry about others taking advantage of you. If you let other people take advantage of you, in the end, you will be the big winner." We explain this philosophy to our people and they understand it conceptually, but in practice, it's difficult to execute. Again and again we demonstrate this to our people by what we do, and over time, they pick up on it and soon they are doing it automatically. If a team member has doubt about whether he is complying with our core values and the DCH Way, we offer a simple question to ask oneself: "If you do something that would appear in the newspaper and you get embarrassed by it, then it is not the right thing to do."

We spend two years implementing the DCH Way internally, and finally we are now confident that we can deliver it consistently. Making a bold decision, we have changed our tag line to "Delivering Customer Happiness," which is a promise we must keep. When people ask us what DCH means, we proudly explain that it stands for Delivering Customer Happiness!

We encourage our teammates to give back to their local communities. We don't solicit business while doing it. We do it because it is the right thing to do. By investing not only financial resources but also human effort and time in the community, it lets people know that we care about them. One group that DCH supports is Students Against Destructive Decisions (SADD), a national organization founded in 1981 that promotes safe teen driving. Being in the automobile business, we are aware that car accidents are the number one cause of death of teens in the U.S. Several thousand are killed annually and hundreds of thousands more are injured. SADD informs teenagers about the effects of destructive decisions that include poor behaviors beyond driving while drinking. It also lets them know about the dangers of taking drugs, texting and of course, it emphasizes that driving safely is the best prevention. SADD distributes a newsletter and program information to its thousands of chapters located in all 50 states. A grassroots organization, it has a small staff at its Marlborough, Massachusetts, headquarters and there are no regional or local offices. DCH provides funding for representatives from different high schools to attend an annual national convention.

DCH dealerships work closely with SADD to take the responsibility in our communities to educate parents and teens about safe driving so responsible decisions are made every time a young person gets behind the wheel of a car. In addition to DCH's financial support, we also donate our human resources to charitable and civic organizations. With our involvement with SADD, our people act as advisors to share real life experience by working with a regional SADD advisor and a faculty advisor at the local school where meetings are conducted with students and attended by our team members. The cost of all advisors are funded by DCH. Team members' participation ranges from discussion of eliminating destructive behavior, to events to bring awareness and do fundraising. They also work on succession planning as the leaders of the chapter graduate.

We challenged students to come up with a creative SADD billboard. Because young people are constantly texting each other, the students adopted a creative theme word, *intexticated*, a play on the word, intoxicated. I suppose that if anyone knows what other kids are thinking, they do! Some of the billboards have *intexticated* on them with tire tread marks showing the danger of driving while texting. DCH has also challenged the students to write essays on destructive driving decisions (it is called D3) and we offer scholarship money for the best essay. We are gratified that the news and advertising media like what we are doing and strongly support us. They interview us, report on our events and give us free billboard and air time. Reuters, the newswire service, displayed our "Intexticated" billboard designs on its Jumbotron in New York City's Time Square at two separate holiday periods.

We are proud of this association and we put up displays at our dealerships to create awareness of what SADD does. We also solicit other automobile dealers to get involved. For instance, I am a board member of the National Automobile Dealers Charitable Foundation, the National Association of Minority Automobile Dealers as well as the Toyota-Lexus Minority Dealers Association and I am constantly trying to convince my fellow members to get involved with teen safe driving.

A few years ago when the economy tanked, the automobile industry was hard hit and we were looking for ways to reduce expenditures. Although our SADD sponsorship runs into the six figures annually, we didn't cut back. Sure, it would have been easy to say, "We're tightening our belt and have to pass this year." But we didn't. Instead we found other areas to save money and never reduced our SADD support. It was simply too good a cause. We gave because it was the right thing to do.

★ Barry's and Bob's Comments ★

One lesson is loud and clear in this story. A company's culture is too important to be left to chance. It takes a concentrated effort to get it right. This is especially true in a large company with multiple locations. Shau-wai Lam had the insight to recognize the value of clearly identifying his company's mission statement and its guiding principles. Once recorded in writing, he didn't stop there. In his words, "Its effectiveness would depend on how well it was implemented." He had to get all of the DCH people spread out in 29 different locations to buy into what he was selling—and yes, he was definitely selling. He wasn't selling a tangible such as an automobile or a truck; instead he was selling a concept, a way to conduct business. To his way of thinking, this was the most important sale he as the Chairman could make. We concur.

Shau-wai first sold the project to Larry Light who could have taken on other much more lucrative assignments. Together with Larry, he then sold it to his management team to give it their full support. Then Shau-wai had to go out to sell all of the people in the DCH organization. Note that he didn't sit in an ivory tower and send emails or elaborate brochures to make his sale. He and his company senior executives made personal visits to tell their story because he wanted everyone in the organization to hear it straight from the top. It was a message that they believed could only be delivered by them.

We commend Shau-wai and the DCH management team for their execution. Sadly, there are many companies that concoct grandiose mission statements that bear little or no resemblance to the way they actually conduct business.

We feel this story has a strong message for every salesperson because it validates that careers are built on honesty and integrity, the cornerstones for success. As Shau-wai makes evident, you don't just tell people what you will do—you must back it up with your actions.

His story reveals that people (and companies) with high principles never compromise their principles. Ever! As Shau-wai says, "Everything else is subject to change. Our organization, our people, our buildings, our products, our strategies may change. But our core values are unchanging." During good times, it's easy to have lofty principles. But when times are tough, in the heat of the day, run-of-the-mill companies are prone to compromise their principles. "We'll do it just this one time," you hear them say, "but only once, never again." Honorable individuals like Shau-wai never give in to temptation and look the other way as a matter of convenience in order to make quarterly or annual sales goals or quotas. Likewise, exceptional salespeople never compromise their principles. A reputable real estate broker doesn't tell a potential home buyer to overstate his income on a bank application in order to qualify for a loan. Nor does she fail to disclose that the seller had previous water damage due to foundation problems. Likewise, a highly principled financial advisor doesn't inform a client only about the upside of an investment. He explains the risks as well. As Henry Ward

Beecher said, "Expedients are for the hour, but principles are for the ages." Live your life and build your career by adhering to high principles, and you will be justly rewarded.

It Takes a Team

Carl Farrell

Executive Vice President, SAS

★ ★ ★

*I*n his role as executive vice president at SAS, Carl Farrell
oversees all sales functions across seven vertical U.S. business
units, including leading all business functions in Canada, Latin
America, and the Caribbean. These markets accounted for 46 percent of SAS's 2010 revenue. With more than 25 years of experience
in the technology industry, spanning sales, consulting, and product
development, he is responsible for delivering consistent revenue
growth while driving the company's overall growth strategy. He
joined SAS in 2002 as the president of SAS Canada. In 2004, Farrell's
responsibilities also grew to include heading up Latin America, which
became SAS's fastest growing region. He was promoted to his current

position in 2006, when he was put in charge of the U.S. sales division. Prior to joining SAS Farrell held senior executive positions at Vignette Corporation, Idiom Technology, JD Edwards, and JBA Holdings. He is a member of the Council of the Americas, an organization that pro- motes economic and social development in the Western Hemisphere.

A business software leader, SAS is a privately held company with annual revenues in excess of $2.4 billion. The company is a leading provider of business analytics solutions, software, and services aimed at solving large-scale business problems. Headquartered in Cary, North Carolina, the company has a workforce of more than 12,000 and is hailed for its reputation for treating employees and customers in a manner that fosters trust and long-term relationships. SAS was ranked number one for two consecutive years in 2010–11 by Fortune magazine on its list of the "Best Companies to Work For" in the U.S.

I n 2004, when I was president of SAS Canada, the Hudson Bay Company (HBC) was in the market to improve its retail operations and looking at new systems to help it do that. At that point, SAS enjoyed a modest relationship with the company—it purchased some software products but not a lot. We wanted to increase our business with it and were up against some strong competitors. As one of the oldest companies in the country and the largest department store, HBC was a prestigious company and a customer we wanted to retain and grow.

At the time, SAS had just purchased Marketmax, a boutique firm with expertise in retail analytics software aimed at analyzing and improving retail operations and forecasting. Marketmax brought a certain sophistication and retail domain expertise to the table that I felt would add value to the services we could provide Hudson Bay.

Our sales team asked me to get involved, and I did, but after reviewing their prepared proposal, I didn't like what I saw. Not one to mince my words, I candidly said, "I believe that if we take our traditional approach, we are not going to have much of a chance."

They looked at me in disbelief. "We don't agree," I was told. "We think we can favorably compete with the competition. Carl, you are wrong on this one."

I said we didn't have the retail domain expertise and pointed out that we didn't speak the language of the customer. "We also don't have the connections with the board," I stressed, "and with a job this size, their people at the highest levels will be involved, including the division presidents, the CEO, CFO, and CIO."

Our sales team was reluctant and could only see the opportunity of getting the business. It was planning to bring in SAS resources from everywhere and believed that everything would fall into place. Hence, it would beat out the competition. I was insistent. "If we are going to have any chance of winning this one," I insisted, "we must do much better. And if we don't, we will lose out."

"What do you suggest we do?" the sales team challenged me.

"We just acquired Marketmax," I explained. "We need to bring in its top executives. I have heard good things about Lori Schafer, its CEO, who has an impressive track record of integrating business intelligence into retailer operations and forecasting.

"I don't personally know Lori, but I want her to work with us on this one, as I'm sure she knows things we don't that will be useful to the customer."

I met with Lori and briefed her on the Hudson Bay opportunity. Interestingly, through her own network, she was already familiar with the situation. "I would like you to put a team together," I said, "and join us in Canada."

She agreed, and with her involvement in place, I tended to the other matter of encouraging multiple sales teams and support staff to work together to meet the customer's need. I thought about the dynamics of having a Canadian sales team and a U.S. sales team that didn't know each other. Understandably the Canadians were resistant, but recognizing the likelihood of them winning the business on their own was zero, it became easier to convince everyone that they must work together and, most importantly, trust each other. This would require an exchange of information by both sides. Next, I had to determine who was going to lead the team.

We had many meetings that involved lengthy conversations along with a lot of pounding of fists on the table by some sales managers before the team decided what was best, and the sales cycle leadership was given to Lori. Her team would play lead, and the Canadians would be the second lead. Nick Lisi, who was the head of sales in Canada at the time, consented to take a back seat, letting Lori take charge. I actually downgraded myself and went through my own process of accepting and learning. Fortunately, Lori is a very nice lady and obviously very smart, so it wasn't difficult for me to make the transition.

The Canadians did the running around and obtained crucial account information, getting the information while Lori quickly established the connection with the senior executives and the HBC board. Once she established a meaningful relationship, the conversations were not about software. Instead, they talked about HBC's values, culture, strategy, business issues, and capabilities. So rather than doing demos, the following several weeks were spent talking about the business plan and the future of Hudson Bay. I emphasize that little was said about the day-to-day transactional activities such as when the store buys something— the focus was on forecasting, space planning, merchandise mix, price optimization, markdown optimization, and some very new techniques. It was about planning and optimization systems. It was about running a good retail business.

We met with the company's most senior people, and we addressed the question "What would the Hudson Bay of the future be like?" Our relationship with the company evolved from SAS being a vendor to having the status of a trusted business advisor. We were being asked questions such as, "How do you advise we do that?" and "Do you think we should do this?" As the sales cycle progressed, the Canadian team got it. Its members saw the difference. As time went on, the trust started to build between the groups, and information and sales strategy began to flow. Later in the process, we did deliver demos and guided HBC's business plans to align to current and future software SAS had in store to develop. Lori systematically went through department by department and reviewed their visions with the Hudson Bay executives. She addressed where it was going to be as a retailer. To her credit, Lori helped piece their vision together into a single vision for the company, which could be enabled by strategically placed technology.

It was beneficial that Lori used to be a retailer. With this background, she was able to look at the multiple modules of software HBC would be buying and help its management build business cases that had return on investment on each of them. With this data, HBC management could present measured results to its board and senior management. Being able to monetize and demonstrate that these projects would self-fund were key differentiators for us winning the deal. Again, this is what helped us to establish trust. Every part of the project we presented had a business case and a return on investment. We looked at the lowest-hanging fruit. Then we analyzed how we could get a return on its investment quickly. We put a lot of effort in making sure that we got quick returns.

We also introduced Hudson Bay people to some of our retail customers in the U.S., and it was helpful for them to visit these companies to see firsthand what we did for them. Although these customers had similar retail operations, they did not have any presence in Canada. The senior people also came to our world headquarters in Cary, North Carolina, to meet with our senior people, including CEO and founder Jim Goodnight.

Then it was time for the Request for Proposal (RFP). We were proposing complex software, and like everything else, nothing is perfect. There were the inevitable speed bumps in the sales cycle, but the strong relationship we built with the company was the key that brought us through. Of course, we had to compete, and we had to prove ourselves. From the technology side and the domain retail side we gained from the Marketmax acquisition, we had a strong internal team. This enabled us to become trusted advisors.

We asked for an open relationship. Then, too, we stated that if we were successful, our objective was to have a partnership for many years. We said that we wanted a minimum five-year contract. It totaled more than $20 million in a five-year period.

★ Barry's and Bob's Comments ★

This story illustrates the value in taking advantage of your company's resources to not only make a sale but also to use it in order to provide maximum benefit to the customer. Sadly, many companies are unable to coordinate their strengths from different areas, and their internal bickering is self-defeating.

This is also a lesson on superb sales management. Neither Farrell nor Lisi let their egos get in the way—they willingly took a back seat to Lori Schafer and gave her the leadership role. This clearly demonstrated how the customer's best interests came first, above their own personal agendas. This was a morale booster for the SAS team, and it sent a message to the customer about what SAS prioritizes. Most importantly, it established a level of trust that elevated SAS to the role of trusted advisor. Winning the trust of customers is what builds long-term relationships and lifelong customers.

Selling to the Big Ego

Barry Farber

President of Farber Training Systems Inc. and The Diamond Group

★ ★ ★

L ike all salespeople, Bob and I love to tell our favorite sales stories. Between the two of us we could fill an entire book of our own—but we didn't give in to the temptation. We limited ourselves to one story each. Here's my story.

★ ★ ★

M any times we pass up or block opportunities because they involve dealing with people whose oversized egos make us feel small . . . if we allow them to.

And some of these people—the ones who act as if they are above us—aren't worth the trouble. In those cases, we're better off simply walking away. But sometimes we need their support—whether for a job, promotion, sale, or other opportunity. Then our relationship with them is key to our own success. How can we handle the egomaniac and still get the results we want?

Don't get me wrong; there are times when a healthy ego, combined with grounded confidence, can help us accomplish many things. I'm talking about people who are grandiose, whose oversized egos can stand in the way of our goals. There's a smart way of dealing with these people—and it starts with listening to them.

Back in 2006 I was meeting with my client, who was working for Six Flags. We first met when he hired me to speak to his sales team at ESPN Television, where he worked at the time. When he came to Six Flags, we were brainstorming about some ideas, and I mentioned that I had just met Robbie Knievel, a motorcycle daredevil and long-distance jumper—and Evel's son. He mentioned the idea of having Robbie jump over one of the theme park's roller coasters. We laughed and thought it would be a great idea to attract people to the park. After a long discussion and obstacles with insurance and logistics, he asked me to see if I could contact Evel Knievel to use his name to build a custom roller coaster. They felt more people would be familiar with his name. It made a lot of sense because the parents who were bringing their kids to Six Flags would remember his jumps from the 1970s. So I reached out to Evel Knievel's bodyguard, and he gave me Evel's phone number.

During my first conversation with Evel Knievel, he asked me why I felt I had the experience to represent him in this deal. A valid question. I told him I had represented internationally known comedian Jackie Mason and gotten him his own TV show, and I also represented Andy Macdonald as his literary agent for his autobiography. Andy was crowned skateboarding's world champion for eight years in a row and the owner of 19 X Game medals—more than any other skater.

Evel wasn't impressed. Instead of ending the conversation there, I let him explain why. He talked about the time he was on the Joey Bishop show and how Joey said that he has the greatest name in show business! Then Evel started going over all the jumps that made him famous. These included his jumps at Caesars Palace, Snake River Canyon, and all the live Wide World of Sports events on ABC television. He said, "Barry, do you know that I own all the rights to all my jump footage on TV? Nobody does that!"

I realized I could go on and on about my past and present accomplishments and they would not be as important to Evel as understanding and listening to all his accomplishments and what made him a daredevil legend. After listening to his list of reasons on why he would be the perfect name for a wild and exciting roller coaster (and he explained it had always been a dream of his to have a roller coaster named after him), I realized that no matter what I said about me, it was all about him. Tony Wainwright, one of my mentors who passed away several years ago, always said when things are not going your way in a certain situation, just listen. Just stop talking and start understanding the other side and the bigger picture. Nobody ever listened themselves out of a sale. So that's what I did.

Then, when he stopped talking and asked why I still felt I was qualified to represent him, I said, "When I was 13, you were my idol. I was sitting on the banana seat of my Schwinn Stingray bicycle, wearing my football helmet, and ready to pedal down my street and jump over five garbage cans using a wooden ramp my father helped me build. It was the fall of 1973, and you were on ABC's Wide World of Sports, about to jump the Grand Canyon. I thought I was you when I was jumping those garbage cans." Without pausing, I concluded, "Today, it would be an honor to represent you."

He then started talking about the Snake River Canyon jump and other reasons why the roller coaster would be a perfect opportunity. Then he and I signed our agreement, and after many back-and-forth conference calls with Six Flags, we made the deal—and the Evel Knievel Roller Coaster was launched at Six Flags St. Louis in the summer of 2008.

✮ Barry's and Bob's Comments ✮

A common mistake of many salespeople is that they talk so much that they talk themselves out of a sale. I confess that I was guilty of that, too, when I was first starting my sales career. But I quickly learned that nobody ever listened himself out of a sale. When Knievel said he wasn't impressed with my clients, I didn't get defensive. My reaction was that he was just testing the waters. Perhaps it was his way to negotiate a deal with me. I wasn't there to win an argument. I was there to make a sale. This is why I listened and let him talk about himself. When you listen to people, you show them that you care about them. I've always believed that people don't care about how much you know until they know how much you care about them.

Once Knievel started to elaborate on his amazing career, I recognized that he had a big ego and let him do the talking. Many people I deal with have big egos. This is especially true with show business personalities, who are in the public eye. It is part of who they are, and you just have to accept it. It comes with the territory. Knievel had one, but it was a well-deserved ego. He was a daredevil jumper and had been credited as being the individual who started extreme arena events. Knievel was known all over the world for his stunts. And when he started bragging about the jumps, that's when I knew I had closed the sale.

How to Avoid "the Slow No"

Robert L. Shook

★ ★ ★

Following the gas shortages that resulted from the Arab-Israeli conflicts, first on the eve of Yom Kippur in 1973 and again in 1978 when the Ayatollah seized control of Iran and turned off the spigot, fuel costs skyrocketed. So did the demand for small, fuel-efficient cars. Domestic automakers were still building gas guzzlers that auto dealers could no longer sell, and the Japanese-built light cars and trucks with excellent fuel efficiency began to sell like hotcakes. It was no contest. American automakers were in a heap of big trouble. Chrysler lost billions, and to stay afloat, the company went to the federal government for a bailout. Ford was also on the brink of bankruptcy, but Chrysler beat them to the punch. The federal government was unwilling to rescue a second automobile company.

In the 1980s, to Ford's credit, the company staged one of the most remarkable turnarounds in American history. What the company did during this period prompted me to explore the possibility of writing a management book on Ford's magnificent comeback. Following a series of telephone calls and letter writing with Jerry Sloan, executive director of public affairs, in the spring of 1989, I made a visit to Ford's world headquarters in Dearborn, Michigan. My purpose was to convince the company's management to extend its full cooperation to me so I could interview Ford employees ranging from assembly line workers to the most senior people in the company, including the CEO and members of the Ford family.

Jerry Sloan was an affable man in his late 50s, and prior to my arrival he had thoroughly scrutinized my credentials. He had read several of my books, liked what he read, and thought that from a public relations viewpoint, the book would be a good thing for the company.

I was in Sloan's office at 10:00 A.M., a half-hour before I was scheduled to meet with the big decision makers. We exchanged pleasantries and had an immediate rapport. "Who will be attending the meeting?" I asked.

"David Scott, our vice president of external affairs, a marketing vice president (I don't remember his name), Don Petersen, our CEO, and a few staff people," Sloan replied. "And I'll be there, too."

"Great," I said. "I appreciate having you set this up for me."

Sloan looked apprehensive. "Bob, there is something I have to tell you," he blurted out. "I'm feeling guilty about having you drive in from Columbus for this meeting because I feel as if you're wasting your time."

"Why so? You got me an audience with Petersen, and I really appreciate it, Jerry."

"This is why I'm feeling guilty, Bob. I was told yesterday late afternoon that Petersen has an important 11:00 meeting that he must attend and to be there on time, he must leave his meeting with you at 10:50, which gives you only 20 minutes to sell him on your book."

"I'll just have to talk faster," I joked.

"It's no laughing matter," Sloan said. "I've seen this scenario a thousand times before. What will happen is that Petersen will stand up sharply at 10:50 and excuse himself from the meeting. On his way out, he'll say, 'Thank you, Bob. We will consider your idea and get back to you.' Whenever this happens, ideas just get buried and never resurface again. You see, while it's a great idea, it won't be considered a top company priority, so we'll never get around to it again. Be assured, Bob, nobody will ever get back to you again. Your book project will be shelved indefinitely. Too bad because I think it has merit. It is something we should do."

"I appreciate your candor," I said, "and it's really good information to know before the meeting."

"It's almost 10:30," Sloan said, looking at his watch. "We don't want to be late. Let's go to the meeting."

Seven of us were seated around a rectangular conference table, and after being introduced to everyone, Sloan said, "I sent a memo around, so you're all familiar with Bob's writing background. I've read several of his books, including two I really enjoyed, one about IBM and another on Honda. He has excellent credentials and wants to tell us why he is interested in writing about Ford. However, he will only do it with our blessings. Bob wants us to give him complete access to talk to anyone at the company he requests to interview."

Sloan turned to me and said, "Okay, Bob, you're up."

I got up from my chair and said in a humble voice, "It is such an honor to be here today, and please excuse me if I seem a bit overwhelmed, but in truth, I am. I want you all to know that my father and my grandfather always drove Fords when I was growing up in Pittsburgh, and ever since I was a child, I've been a huge Ford fan. In my opinion, Ford was the greatest automobile manufacturer in the world. No, let's make that the greatest company in the world. And here I am today, meeting with the key decision makers of Ford Motor Company. I was so excited to be here this morning that I wasn't able to sleep last night."

True, I was laying it on thick, and it sounded mushy. But I knew it was so different from what they were expecting that I had their complete attention. I noticed a few faint smiles, and in particular, one on Petersen. So far so good, I thought to myself.

"I am so appreciative of your time," I continued. "I am so grateful to meet with top decision makers of this great company. What I appreciate so much is that after I present my book project to you, I know that with all the big decisions that are made around here in the scheme of things it's a relatively easy decision to make. This is what I like so much about talking to all of you in this room today. I know that by the time this meeting ends and you have all the facts about my proposal, you will be in a position to say aye or nay, and I'll know exactly where I stand. We'll either move forward on this, or it will end right here. I know I won't be given the 'slow no.'

"Incidentally, this is a major reason why Ford was on my radar screen regarding a book to write. Over the years, I've worked with other large corporations that were loaded with such bureaucracy that I simply refused to deal with them. They run you through a bureaucratic shuffle you wouldn't believe! Consequently, I've vowed to never put myself in such a position. Frankly, at this stage in my career, I'm not into grief. There are just so many good books that I want to write that there is never a shortage of what I will do next. So if I even sense a company is going to give me the slow no, I simply walk away and look for another company to write about."

Nobody said a word. I studied their reaction, glanced at my watch and continued. I had approximately 14 minutes until Petersen would be headed out the door, and from my prospective that would be the end of the meeting. Without missing a beat, I distributed a chapter outline to everyone in the room while explaining why I thought the book would be an effective marketing tool for the company. Then I conducted a five-minute question-and-answer session.

At exactly 10:50, Petersen stood up and announced, "I have to excuse myself but before I leave, I see no reason why we can't give Bob the go-ahead so he can get started with his book. Does anyone disagree?"

Everyone nodded in approval and Petersen said, "Jerry, you'll be our lead man on this book." He then said to me, "Bob, we appreciate your interest in our company and we're looking forward to working with you. Please be sure to let me know if there is anything you need from me."

As we walked down the corridor on our way to Sloan's office, he said, "Bob, I don't know what happened in there, but before the meeting, I didn't think you had a snowball's chance in hell of getting Petersen aboard like you did. I'm looking forward to working with you on your book."

I just smiled and didn't say a word.

✭ Barry's and Bob's Comments ✭

What Jerry Sloan didn't pick up was that I started closing the sale with my opening remarks. Of course, it was intended to be subtle so he and the others were not aware that I was setting them up to take action following my presentation. Had I waited until the end of the meeting to say that I expected a commitment, it could have backfired because it would have been viewed as a high-pressure tactic. However, contrary to what most people think, the close of a sale doesn't necessarily occur at the end of the presentation. You can close a sale at any time. In this case, I let it be known that I expected them to make an immediate decision because I would not tolerate getting the runaround. Sloan had warned me in advance that if Petersen said he would think it over and get back to me, it would be a dead end, and I took his comment very seriously. I abandoned the visual presentation I brought with me even though it took several hours preparing charts and diagrams. Instead I chose to spend the limited time I had with Petersen in the room by letting it be known that I wouldn't tolerate the slow no and wasn't interested in working with a company that was unable to make a decision on the spot.

In my early days as a life insurance agent, I used this same tactic when I called on mom-and-pop businesses. Then, too, I set them up by saying to small-business owners, "I like working with business owners because like you they are capable of making decisions. They don't have to talk it over with the wives. They are businesspeople who make independent decisions every day." Note that people are people—it doesn't matter if they run a little corner grocery store or a giant international company like the Ford Motor Company. Big or small, they have the same emotions and egos. By flattering people on their ability to be decisive, they are less apt to procrastinate. Why? They don't want to disappoint you by failing to live up to your expectations. This is why this selling technique can be used with people at all levels. Just remember, people are people—it doesn't matter if they are powerful and rich or of modest means. Good selling techniques are effective with people in all walks of life. Let them know you won't tolerate the slow no, and you will gain their respect—and, most important, you close the sale!

Epilogue

★ ★ ★

Conducting interviews and writing this book was a priceless education and an enjoyable experience from start to finish. We met some fascinating storytellers, each delightful, charming, and enthusiastic. Their stories were filled with innovative sales techniques that can be applied by salespeople in all fields. The good news is that you don't have to be a salesperson to benefit from these wonderful stories, nor do you have to work directly with customers. You can have a nonsales job and apply the lessons that appear throughout the book. That's because, no matter what your job entails, to be successful, you must be able to sell.

When you graduate from college, you probably will have to compete against ten applicants for the same job. On paper, their résumés are pretty much the same—their grade average, school activities, summer jobs, and so on. The tie-breaker is that you must be the one who can best sell yourself during an interview. The same thing happens when you apply for a promotion and compete against three or four other candidates. Likewise, to succeed in corporate America, you must sell your boss, and if you *are* the boss, you must sell your people. If you're the CEO and you don't sell your management team to win their support, a project has two strikes against it before it ever starts. Similarly, as the chairman, you must sell the members of the board of directors. You see, every one of us is continually selling. It's not just the sales reps out there, pounding the pavement, calling on customers.

Like any profession, sales professionals never stop learning, and one thing is certain in today's fast-paced world—things are changing continually. The only thing that's constant is change. If you don't keep current, you're living in the past. As Warren Buffet said, "If past history were all there was to the game, the richest people would be librarians."

In all fields, successful people are engaged in a lifelong educational program, continually learning and keeping up-to-date on what's going on in their industry: new products on the drawing board, what their competitors are doing, the latest happenings in technology, and so on. During our visits to the sales experts we met while doing interviews for this book, we observed that to stay ahead of the competition you can never stand still. You either go forward, or you go backward. Lewis Carroll, who wrote *Alice in Wonderland*, expressed this thought when the Red Queen advised Alice, "Now, here you see, it takes all the running you can do to keep in the same place. If you want to get somewhere else, you must run twice as fast!" This reminds us that in order to go forward we must never stop learning.

We realize that with all of the news reported by the media and on the internet, every one of us is being bombarded with an incredible amount of information and in such high daily volumes that it's extremely time-consuming to absorb everything we need to know. Then there are all the books we need to read to stay on top of things. Having known thousands of business leaders and top salespeople over the years, we recognized that much of this required reading material is technical and doesn't always hold one's interest. This is why we chose a format filled with stories that would be short, interesting, and fun to read. Our goal is that you enjoy the book and learn from it. We hope that you did and, most importantly, that it enhances your career.

As all salespeople know, long-term success comes from satisfied customers who place repeat orders and refer others to them. The same is true with writers; we want our readers to read our past and future books and thrive on word-of-mouth referrals. Referrals from satisfied customers are essential to salespeople, and as writers, we depend on referrals from satisfied readers!

Oops! There we go again, always selling. As they say, once a salesman, always a salesman. Yes, we are both salesmen and proud of it. We take great pride in having presented you with our collection of the best sales tales ever told. We hope you enjoyed every one of them.

About the Authors

★ ★ ★

★ Robert L. Shook ★

New York Times Bestselling Author

Career: Author

Prior to being a full-time writer for the past 31 years: founder and chairman of the board of Shook Associates Corporation and American Executive Life Insurance Company.

Honors: Author of five *New York Times* bestsellers. Guest on more than 1,000 radio and TV shows including *The Today Show, The David Susskind Show, The Sally Jessy Raphael Show, the Disney Channel, CNN*. Books have been featured on *60 Minutes, Good Morning America, Larry King Live*, and others. *Mary Kay on People*

Management was studied at the Harvard Business School. Member of board of directors of Value City Department Stores, 1991–2002.

Public Service/Community Service: Chairman of the board-American Cancer Society (Franklin County) 2000–2002; ACS board member (1985–2002); 1994 Volunteer of the Year-American Cancer Society; past board member of Opera/Columbus, Players Theater of Columbus, and member of the Columbus Adopt-a-School Program.

Selected Publications: Author of 55 published books—54 non-fiction, one fiction, all selected by author. Published in more than 40 languages. Titles of books include: *The IBM Way; Honda: An American Success Story; Turnaround: the New Ford Motor Company; Miracle Medicines; The Greatest Sales Stories Ever Told; The Perfect Sales Presentation; Hardball Selling' The Customer Rules' Predatory Marketing; Longaberger* (NYT #1 bestseller); and *Mary Kay on People Management* (NYT #1 bestseller); and *Heart & Soul*. The author's one work of fiction, *The Pep Talk*, will be released as a major motion picture in 2013. His work in progress is entitled *Brands that Never Die: What I Learned from Bogie, Elvis, Marilyn and James Dean (and Hundreds of Other Dead Celebrities I Represent)*, a book collaboration with Mark Roesler, Founder/CEO of CMG Worldwide.

Contact information: email: shookbooks@aol.com or website: www. robertlshook.webs.com.

⋆ Barry Farber ⋆
President of Farber Training Systems Inc.
and The Diamond Group.

For more than 20 years Barry Farber has trained and consulted Fortune 500 corporations, business owners, professional athletes, and entertainers, helping them market their products and land more deals. He has trained more than 500,000 salespeople and helped companies increase their sales by more than 50 percent while gaining access to millions of dollars of new business. Some of his clients include AT&T, American Express, BMW, Chase, ESPN/ABC Sports, Merck, Nestle Waters, State Farm Insurance, Toshiba, UPS, and Verizon.

He was rated as the "hottest speaker of the year" by *Successful Meetings* magazine and is the bestselling author of 12 books in more than 25 foreign languages with over one million copies sold. Some of his books include: *The 12 Cliches of Selling and Why They Work, Barry Farber's Guide to Handling Sales Objections, Superstar Sales Secrets, Superstar Sales Manager's Secrets, Diamond Power, Diamond in the Rough,* and *State of the Art Selling.*

Barry hosted more than 400 Radio and TV shows in New York City, Washington, and on the Comcast Television Network. Some of his guests have included: Don Rickles, Barbara Mandrell, Evander Holyfield, Dave Thomas (founder of Wendy's), Rita Rudner, and Jim McCann of 1800Flowers. In addition to hosting his own show, Farber has been interviewed on CBS, NBC, ABC, FOX, CNBC, and CNN. He has also been featured in *Ad Week, Investors Business Daily, Newsday, U.S. News & World Report, Variety,* and *The New York Times.*

Barry is a columnist for *Inc.* magazine and has written more than 500 columns for magazines such as *Entrepreneur* and *Sales and Marketing Management.* He can also be seen as a regular guest on QVC selling out unique and innovative inventions since 1997.

What makes Barry's consulting and training programs unique and practical are the real-world applications he shares from his day-to-day activities. He was the broker and agent for the $7 million Evel Knievel roller coaster that Six Flags Theme Parks launched in the summer of 2008; winner of three Telly Awards; and nominated for an Emmy as the executive producer of the *Jackie Mason Television Show;* co-inventor and marketer of the FoldzFlat® Pen, selling millions in the promotional, direct response, and retail markets; and Black Belt Weapons Regional and National Tournament Champion where he incorporates his martial arts experience into his presentations with an entertaining and inspirational message.

Contact Information
Email: barry@barryfarber.com
Phone: (973) 535-9400
Website: www.barryfarber.com

Index

★ ★ ★